Low Hanging Fruit

In the Garden of Life

Jojen Jose

AF583226

INDIA · SINGAPORE · MALAYSIA

Copyright © Jojen Jose 2023
All Rights Reserved.

ISBN 979-8-89067-835-5

This book has been published with all efforts taken to make the material error-free after the consent of the author. However, the author and the publisher do not assume and hereby disclaim any liability to any party for any loss, damage, or disruption caused by errors or omissions, whether such errors or omissions result from negligence, accident, or any other cause.

While every effort has been made to avoid any mistake or omission, this publication is being sold on the condition and understanding that neither the author nor the publishers or printers would be liable in any manner to any person by reason of any mistake or omission in this publication or for any action taken or omitted to be taken or advice rendered or accepted on the basis of this work. For any defect in printing or binding the publishers will be liable only to replace the defective copy by another copy of this work then available.

CONTENTS

ACKNOWLEDGEMENT

I am immensely grateful for the completion of this book that speaks about happiness, which stands as a testament to my study in the pursuit of understanding and embracing the essence of true happiness. Throughout this remarkable journey, I have been blessed to receive support, guidance, and inspiration from countless individuals and institutions that have played an integral role in shaping both my work and my personal growth.

First and foremost, I extend my heartfelt appreciation to my family, whose unwavering encouragement and belief in me have been a constant source of strength throughout this extensive endeavor. Their presence and support have nurtured my spirit, empowering me to tread this path with unwavering determination and resilience.

I am profoundly grateful to my close companions whose support and candid sharing of experiences have brought valuable insight to this book. Their openness, honesty, and willingness to contribute have illuminated the diverse facets of happiness, enabling me to delve into its depths and unearth profound insights.

I extend my heartfelt thanks to my mentors and advisors, whose expertise, guidance, and wisdom have shaped my understanding of happiness and fueled my intellectual curiosity. Their invaluable insights, thought-provoking discussions, and constructive feedback have propelled me forward and broadened the horizons of my research.

I am indebted to the institutions that have provided me with the necessary resources, facilities, and opportunities to pursue my study on happiness. Their commitment to fostering knowledge and innovation has been instrumental in shaping the framework of my research and enabling its fruition.

I am grateful to the numerous authors, scholars, and researchers whose works have served as a source of inspiration, challenging me to think critically and contributing to the foundation upon which this book is built. Their dedication to the study of happiness has expanded the collective understanding of this intricate subject matter.

Finally, I extend my heartfelt appreciation in advance to the readers of this book. It is my sincere hope that this book serves as a guide, igniting a spark of introspection and guiding individuals on their own unique journey towards happiness and fulfillment.

This acknowledgement is a humble recognition of the collaborative nature of knowledge and the interdependence of individuals in the pursuit of understanding happiness. The completion of this book would not have been possible without the support and contributions of those mentioned above, and for that, I am eternally grateful.

With profound gratitude

Jojen Jose

PREFACE

In the pages of this book, you'll find a powerful tool that can guide you on your journey of self-discovery and personal growth. Think of it as a supportive companion, always by your side, offering valuable insights and encouragement for all your endeavors.

The aim of this book is to reach as many people as possible by presenting information in a simple and accessible way. To enhance clarity while maintaining simplicity, the book includes graphics and anecdotes. These elements have been added to make the content easier to understand and engage with.

What makes this book special is that it draws from my own life experiences and the lessons I've learned along the way. As you read through these pages, you'll discover practical wisdom and real-life implementations that have made a profound impact on my life.

It is my heartfelt wish that this *self-help book* becomes a source of inspiration and empowerment for you. May it spark new ideas, ignite your passions, and lead you towards a more fulfilling and meaningful life. You have the power to shape your own life, and with the guidance within these chapters, you'll be better equipped to overcome challenges and welcome success.

As you dive into the contents of this book, you might encounter moments where what you read contradicts with the beliefs you've held for a long time. When that happens, I encourage you to keep an open mind, continue reading until the very end and follow the steps presented within these pages.

Change can be challenging, especially when it challenges our deeply rooted beliefs. But, it is in those moments of discomfort that true growth takes root. By staying committed and exploring the ideas shared in this book, you'll start to notice a significant shift in your life – one that aligns more closely with your true purpose.

In order to emphasize several crucial elements of life, I have reinstated them to enhance clarity and comprehension.

Transformation is a process, and it takes time. Allow yourself the space to absorb and integrate the wisdom imparted here. Each step you take brings you closer to unlocking your fullest potential and discovering the path that resonates with you.

Why This Book is Needed and How It Came Into Being

Throughout my own life, I encountered numerous sources of advice and perspectives on improving one's personal life. While these insights came from various directions, I often felt the need for a consolidated and reliable guide that could be easily accessed in one place. It became clear to me that I wasn't alone in this search; many others also sought a trustworthy resource for personal growth.

Driven by my own desire to find such a guide, I embarked on a journey of exploration. I delved into various areas of human life, seeking wisdom from a diverse range of people. Their valuable input and experiences helped shape the foundation of this self-help book, which I envisioned as a personal coach for anyone seeking change and empowerment.

This book is the culmination of collective efforts and shared knowledge. It is the product of real-life experiences, struggles, and triumphs. As I poured energy into crafting these pages, I couldn't help but reflect on how this knowledge has profoundly impacted my life and the lives of those around me.

And now, with great excitement and optimism, I present this book to you. I am confident that it will serve as a guiding compass, leading you towards transformation and growth, just as it has done for me and many others connected to this journey.

I am sure this book will become your reliable guide, journeying alongside you during trials and times of self-exploration. Let it equip you to navigate the unexpected paths of life and direct you toward a destination of fulfillment and meaning.

To Whom This Book is Meant For

As you set sail into the pages of this book, let me clarify who it is meant for. This book is a treasure trove for people of all age segments, except the very young kids. Whether you're in your teenage years, young adulthood, or even a seasoned adult, you are invited to join this journey of self-discovery.

Parents, although this book is not specifically targeted at kids, it can still offer valuable insights for you. By delving into its wisdom, you can gain knowledge that will aid you in imparting good parenting to your children. It is a tool to foster understanding and connection within your family, guiding you in nurturing a constructive and supportive environment.

Throughout our lives, from the moment we enter the transformative phase of puberty to every chapter beyond, we all share a common pursuit that unites us as human beings. It is the quest for meaning, happiness, and purpose that makes our existence truly meaningful.

How to Read This Book

I'm delighted to tell you how to approach this book and make the most of its contents. This book is designed with two distinct sections, each serving a unique purpose in your journey of self-discovery.

Section A is all about increasing your awareness about life. It offers insights, reflections, and thought-provoking ideas that will encourage you to contemplate and gain a deeper understanding of your own existence. Through this section, you'll find clarity and a new perspective on the beautiful life that is already unfolding around you.

Once you've explored the realm of awareness in Section A, move on to Section B. Here, you'll discover a wealth of practices and methods that empower you to fully experience the beauty of this already happening life. These practical tools will help you integrate newfound knowledge into your daily experiences, transforming your life into a more enriching and fulfilling one.

As you read through both sections, take your time to reflect and absorb the wisdom shared within. Feel free to pause and revisit sections that resonate with you deeply. This book is your guide on a continuous journey of growth, so allow yourself the freedom to explore at your own pace.

For Example

If you already have a good understanding of the principal aspects of life, you may want to breeze through Section A and place more focus on the practical implementations provided in Section B. These actionable steps will help you incorporate the knowledge you already possess into your daily life, leading to constructive changes and personal development.

Now, there might be times in life when you find yourself caught in situations filled with chaos and confusion. If that resonates with you, I recommend reading the lesson on "Psychological Resolution" and considering the "Appreciation Ritual", both found in Section B. These tools can bring solace and clarity, helping you navigate through challenging times.

Furthermore, if you are facing relationship issues with your spouse, Section A holds valuable insights on gender-wise prominence, explored in "The Enigma Unveiled." Once you gain understanding from that section, move on to Section B to delve into "Embrace the Inner Majesty." These practices can aid in nurturing a harmonious and fulfilling relationship.

Regardless of your current situation, I wholeheartedly recommend delving into the pages of this book. By doing so, you will uncover a profound understanding of life, enabling you to cultivate awareness and make informed decisions for your overall well-being. These pages will undoubtedly prove transformative, guiding you towards a more fulfilling and balanced existence. So, I encourage each one of you to set out on this enlightening journey of self-discovery and growth. Your well-being deserves nothing less than your full engagement with the invaluable insights offered in these words.

To experience the full potential of the 'Happiness pathfinders' in section 'B,' it is crucial to follow the designated order outlined in the index. These practices can profoundly transform your life and yield meaningful rewards.

This book is meant to be your supportive guide throughout life's journey. Feel free to explore the sections that echo with you most deeply and revisit them whenever you need inspiration and guidance.

Purpose of Stories

This book is adorned with a collection of short stories and anecdotes. These stories serve a special purpose - to bring greater clarity to the concepts of the life skills discussed throughout the book.

I've carefully chosen each story to complement the related life skill, making it easier for you to grasp the essence of these invaluable lessons. The stories are presented in a simple and engaging manner, designed to enrich the content and make it easily understandable.

As you read through these stories and anecdotes, you'll find yourself drawn into the narratives, and through them, you'll gain deeper insights into the principles and practices shared in this book. These have the power to touch you and leave a lasting impact on your understanding of the life skills we explore together.

Let these tales serve as guiding lights, illuminating your path towards personal growth and transformation. Welcome the wisdom they hold and let them inspire you to make constructive changes in your life.

Benefits of This Book

This self-help book offers guidance that directs you towards sustainable happiness while providing tools to tackle challenges with resilience. Its pages hold insights to foster personal growth, emotional intelligence, and a creative mindset, enabling you to navigate life's complexities more confidently and find a deeper sense of contentment.

Let us adopt this valuable resource and commence on a path of self-discovery and empowerment. Together, we will navigate life's challenges, drawing strength from the guidance offered by this book. With determination and openness, let us witness remarkable changes in our lives that lead us towards a more fulfilling and purposeful existence.

"It is said that nothing is impossible but there is one thing which is really impossible - Good life though poor lifestyle"

SECTION A

AWARENESS: LET US DISCOVER OUR TRUE SELF

CHAPTER 1

PURPOSE OF LIFE

"Happiness is the meaning and the purpose of life, the whole aim and end of human existence."

– ***Aristotle***

Life can get pretty hectic and overwhelming sometimes, right? In the fast-paced world we live in, it's easy to see people around us constantly chasing after different things, all in the pursuit of happiness.

And that brings us to the concept of happiness. Happiness isn't just a fleeting feeling that comes and goes like a passing breeze. It's about something deeper, enduring and sustainable that we often call "Joy."

Let's clear up a common misconception - Happiness as instant gratification. Know those moments when we feel an instant rush of pleasure from something we get or experience? That's instant gratification. It can happen within a few moments or even last for a few days. And here's the tricky part – it's so realistic that we often confuse it with true happiness.

But real happiness goes beyond these fleeting moments. It's about finding joy and contentment that lasts, even during life's ups and downs - a steady flame that keeps burning inside us, providing warmth and comfort no matter what challenges we face.

To truly grasp this sustainable happiness, we need to look within ourselves and become more aware. It's about understanding our true desires and values, free from the influence of our surroundings.

Our environment plays a significant role in how we perceive happiness and the choices we make to achieve it. From a young age, we're bombarded with societal norms and expectations that shape our goals and aspirations. Messages from various sources and societal comparisons can deceive us into thinking that happiness is synonymous with owning material goods only or reaching specific life goals.

But here's the secret to unlocking genuine happiness – it starts with self-reflection. By taking the time to know ourselves better, we discover what truly matters to us on a deeper level. We uncover our passions, values, and aspirations, allowing us to make choices that align with our inner selves.

Often, I talk to people about the purpose of life, and many times, they tell me that they think the most important thing is to take care of their family, community, and the environment. Once, I asked someone the same question, and they said their main goal in life is to help their family do well, especially making sure their kids have a good future. I asked them if all the time, effort, and money they put into this made them get back something equally good. They didn't even need to think and quickly said, "feeling happy". This is a moment when we realize what we're really meant to do in life. It seems that all the things we do come from a big desire to feel happy - a very strong wish. This strong wish helps us live lives that are important and have meaning.

When we live with purpose and meaning, our actions take on a transformative quality. It's not just about chasing personal gratification but seeking fulfillment in our journey towards sustainable happiness.

However, the pursuit of happiness is an ongoing endeavor, not a one-time destination. While it's essential to strive for happiness, we must also find a balance in our lives. An excessive focus on achieving momentary pleasure can lead to stress and dissatisfaction.

Taking care of ourselves, nurturing our relationships, and finding moments of calm reflection are vital for sustaining our pursuit of happiness in a healthy way. It's about caring for our overall well-being and finding joy in the little things as well as the big achievements.

Now, here's a vital ingredient in sustaining happiness – it's our mindset. Sustainable happiness doesn't solely depend on the happening of any particular event, it's about how we perceive and respond to life's events.

How we think affects how we live, and the choices we make in life determine if we're truly happy in the long run. Knowing the difference between instant gratification and long-lasting happiness plays a vital role in this endeavor.

Life is an incredible adventure, and each day offers us countless possibilities to experience happiness. So, take a moment to ponder what brings us true joy and fulfillment.

We need to be brave and explore what really makes us happy. Let's uncover the treasure trove of happiness that lies within us and create a life that resonates with our true selves. It's a journey well worth taking.

Chapter 2

SUBLIMINAL STORYLINE

"What we are today comes from our thoughts of yesterday, and our present thoughts build our life of tomorrow. Our life is the creation of our mind".

– Gautam Buddha

Let's delve into the fascinating world of subliminal storylines and explore the hidden power of our thoughts.

Our mind is a complex realm, where conscious and subconscious processes intertwine like a dance. While we often focus on our conscious thoughts and decisions, there's a whole secret world beneath the surface – the subconscious mind. And it's this hidden realm that profoundly influences how we behave, what we believe, and how we perceive the world around us.

In this journey of awareness, we need to cultivate knowledge about its intricacies.

So, what exactly is the subconscious mind? Think of it as an immense reservoir brimming with thoughts, emotions, memories, and automatic behaviours. This hidden world profoundly influences our habits, attitudes, and responses to everything we experience. While the conscious mind handles our rational thinking and decision-making, the subconscious mind holds significant sway over our overall behaviour.

When we're born, we come equipped with some built-in programs in our subconscious that help us survive. As we grow, our experiences, education, and environment become the architects of our subconscious mind. It's a grand library of beliefs, thoughts, and behavioural patterns that shape who we are.

The subconscious mind is like a brilliant puzzle master. It pieces together information, memories, and emotions, creating the foundation for our thoughts. It's not just logical; it's also super creative. It can make intuitive leaps and help us solve problems in clever ways.

During our formative years, particularly childhood and adolescence, the subconscious mind is like a sponge, soaking up everything around us. It's in this period that we're most receptive to external influences, like a blank canvas waiting to be painted with knowledge and values. Our family, other people around and surroundings all leave their marks on this canvas, forming the foundation of our thoughts and beliefs.

Though sometimes, the subconscious mind can be a sneaky troublemaker. It might hold on to limiting beliefs or bleak thought patterns that keep us from reaching our full potential. We can shine a bright light on these shadows and uncover hidden treasures of constructive change and personal growth. By working with our conscious thoughts, we can unlock new realms of creativity, insight, personal growth and break free from those limiting beliefs and soaring towards a more fulfilling and purposeful life.

Inner Revelation

Let's discover the amazing strength that exists within each of us – the power of human beings. This power is not something from the outside or magical; it is inside us. But to use this potential, we first need to know about it. And to understand this, we must explore the fascinating world of how our minds work.

Understanding how our minds and emotions function helps us unravel the complexities of our thoughts, feelings, and actions. By knowing these things, we can unlock the hidden potential inside us.

This understanding is crucial in every aspect of our life experiences – from our thought processes and learning methods to our interactions with others and our functioning in diverse environments.

Once we know about our internal strength, we can start using it for personal growth and development. It gives us the ability to face challenges, overcome obstacles, and achieve our dreams.

Let's explore the fascinating aspects of life connected to psychology, which involves understanding how our mind and emotions work. By delving into these psychological aspects, we can uncover hidden gems of knowledge and realize the boundless potential that lies ahead.

Here is one interesting way to understand its importance.

"We are born with "Biology"
Enter the world of "Sociology"
Spend our lives learning "Economics"
But often overlook "Psychology"
which is the key to our Happiness"

Primal Desires

It is the fascinating world of human primal desires. These are basic needs that are a part of who we are, deep in our subconscious minds.

As human beings, we all have primal desires that are deeply ingrained in our nature. These basic desires are the fundamental needs that drive our actions and behaviours. They are the very essence of what makes us human. Some of these primal desires include the need for food, water, shelter, and safety, which are essential for our survival. We also have a natural yearning for connection and belonging, seeking companionship and forming relationships with others. Additionally, the desire for growth and self-improvement pushes us to learn, explore, and evolve as individuals. Understanding these primal desires can help us navigate life with a deeper sense of purpose and fulfillment.

We have these powerful instincts within us, driving our actions and desires. These primal desires are the scripts that guide us, and there are ten of them that we often talk about:

- **Survival**: It's our natural instinct to ensure our own well-being and survival. We seek things like air, food, water, and shelter to keep ourselves healthy.
- **Protection**: We all want to feel safe and secure. This means protecting ourselves from harm, both physical and emotional. We desire a stable and predictable environment to feel secure.
- **Freedom**: We crave the freedom to be ourselves, which includes the physical and mental autonomy to express thoughts, pursue goals, and embrace dreams.
- **Comfort**: We naturally seek comfort – both physically and mentally. We want to relax and avoid any pain or discomfort.
- **Relationship**: Humans are social beings, and we crave connections with others. We desire companionship, care, and meaningful relationships.

- **Exploration**: We are so curious about the world around us, because of our natural drive to explore and learn. We love to seek new experiences and expand our knowledge.
- **Appreciation**: Being kind and appreciating ourselves and others is a special desire within us. It's a force that connects us with others and helps us grow and evolve as individuals.
- **Pleasure**: We all love to feel good and experience enjoyable things. Whether it's emotional, sensory, or intellectual pleasure, seeking it is a natural desire.
- **Success**: Achieving things and growing as individuals is another powerful desire. We want to acquire accomplishments, master skills, and pursue our dreams.
- **Likeability**: We want to be liked and accepted by others. It's important for us to feel validated, have social status, and be respected by our peers.

In our exploration of the captivating world of primal desires, we have uncovered the hidden gears that shape our thoughts and actions. These fundamental needs, nestled deep within our subconscious minds, guide us as we journey through life. From the instinct to survive and seek protection to the longing for freedom, comfort, and meaningful relationships, these desires form the very essence of our human nature. Understanding these primal desires not only enriches our self-awareness but also empowers us to pursue personal growth, forge authentic connections, and find purpose in our endeavours. As we navigate our path, we need to honour these instincts as valuable compass points, illuminating the way to a more fulfilling and purposeful existence.

Comfort Zone

Now that we have delved into the concept of primal desires, let's delve deeper into one of the crucial aspects - comfort. This innate need for comfort often creates what we call a 'comfort zone.' Imagine it as a safe and cozy place where we feel at ease, shielded from potential discomfort or challenges.

In past generations, our comfort zones were not as prominent since people were constantly engaged in day-to-day struggles for survival. However, in our modern times, with an abundance of resources and conveniences, the comfort zone has transformed into a significant obstacle in our pursuit of personal growth and exploration.

Comfort zones are akin to vast chasms that can gradually widen and deepen without our awareness. The more we surrender to our comfort, the more we reinforce its boundaries, creating a logical fallacy that convinces us it's the right place to be. We develop a skewed sense of justification, not realizing that our minds are playing tricks on us.

These logical fallacies act as the tools to construct and solidify our comfort zones. At first glance, they appear as convincing beliefs that keep us tethered to our comfort, but they are fundamentally flawed. The problem lies in our inability to perceive these fallacies and the chasm they create when we lack self-awareness.

By breaking free from the comfort zone, we open the door to fulfilling the subsequent seven primal desires, surmounting hurdles that may otherwise impede their progression. This empowering journey not only nurtures growth and fulfillment but also preserves the vital core of the former three desires.

Embracing discomfort, uncertainty, and stepping out of our comfort zone allows us to embark on new adventures, discover hidden talents, and unlock our true potential.

Comfort zones can take various forms, and they can be found in different aspects of our lives. Here are a few examples of comfort zones in various categories:

- **Knowledge Comfort Zones**: This comfort zone can manifest in various areas of our lives. In linguistics, it's evident when we cling to familiar languages and avoid learning new ones. Similarly, in science, comfort zones arise when we refuse to explore or accept new ideas and theories. For example, in the realm of technology, we resist adopting new innovations, preferring to stick with what we already know.

- **Habit Comfort Zones**: There are various types. The *virtue signaling comfort zone* entails engaging in actions or behaviours primarily to seek approval or praise from others, lacking genuine belief in them. It reflects a desire to be seen as virtuous without a sincere commitment to the principles or causes involved. Similarly, the *false optimism comfort zone* involves perpetually maintaining a positive outlook, even when confronted with harsh realities, thus evading necessary confrontations or adjustments. This attitude may lead to a detachment from reality and hinder personal growth and problem-solving capabilities.
- **Terrestrial Comfort Zones:** Comfort zones can extend to various physical settings, including the *home comfort zone*, where individuals tend to stay within the confines of their familiar surroundings, shying away from new places and experiences. Similarly, the *room comfort zone* keeps people confined to specific spaces where they feel secure and comfortable, hesitating to venture beyond. In the professional context, the *workplace comfort zone* limits individuals to familiar tasks and routines, avoiding challenges and new responsibilities.
- **Belief Comfort Zones**: Such as the *default conditioned mindset comfort zone*, occur when individuals cling to beliefs and opinions simply because they have been ingrained since childhood or influenced by the environment, without subjecting them to critical examination.
- **Receiving end Comfort Zone**: Most people, due to a consumption mindset, push themselves unknowingly into the comfort zone of receiving. In their conditioning, it is ingrained that through consumption only will they attain their life's purpose. The adverse effect of this zone is that people gradually move away from the giving mindset, which impedes gratitude in their lives, leading to an uninteresting life.

Comfort zones in any of these categories can limit personal growth and hinder our ability to explore new opportunities and experiences. Challenging these comfort zones requires a willingness to question and reevaluate our beliefs, fostering a more open and adaptable mindset that encourages personal growth and a deeper understanding.

For example, we see a person who confidently praises space technology, yet their lack of competence in their primary responsibility is apparent. In today's world, acquiring knowledge has become effortless due to its abundant availability. However, this knowledge only scratches the surface of their personality. Deep inside lies a significant delay, which is the true cause of their shortcomings and setbacks.

Creating awareness about the comfort zone is of utmost importance in today's world to empower our pursuit of happiness. When we recognize and understand the limitations imposed by our comfort zones, we can take intentional steps to step out of them.

Sensory Intelligence

Let's explore the intriguing concept of sensory intelligence, which communicates through two fundamental languages: pain and pleasure. These languages play crucial roles in ensuring our survival, protection, and overall well-being, shaping our entire lives around them.

Pain acts as a protective mechanism, alerting our minds to potential threats and dangers. Even when faced with a small pain, our minds automatically become vigilant, as it is a natural mechanism to safeguard our lives. On the other hand, pleasure ensures our basic survival needs are met, guiding us to seek things like food and comfort. Our minds are always attentive to possible sources of pleasure, drawing our attention towards them.

We experience pain and pleasure at the body level, such as feeling physical pain from an injury or enjoying the pleasure of eating something delicious. However, these sensations can also be triggered by our minds, regardless of any obvious cause. When feelings are initiated by the mind, we call them "emotions". Sadly, pain triggered through emotions can be particularly destructive, as unawareness can turn pain into prolonged suffering. Many times, the pain created by the mind is imaginary, as our minds struggle to differentiate between reality and imagination, leading to the manifestation of pain.

Similarly, pleasure can also be triggered through the mind. We have the remarkable ability to imagine both pain and pleasure through our innate power of imagination. This principle forms the basis of various self-reflection practices, which harness the power of our imagination to foster relaxation and beneficial experiences.

In ancient times, when our ancestors relied heavily on these basic languages, pain alerted them to potential dangers, triggering instinctual responses like flight, fight, or hiding to protect themselves. At the same time, the pursuit of pleasure, particularly food, drove them to hunt for sustenance. These languages were primarily focused on meeting their physical needs during that time.

Today, our survival, protection, and comfort needs are often met mechanically. However, our primitive tendencies continue to operate in the background, as we remain largely unaware of these basic languages. Consequently, these unconscious triggers can lead to damaging emotions that affect our mental well-being.

To minimize the harmful effects of such emotions, self-awareness becomes the key. By understanding these basic languages and how they can influence our emotions, we gain the power to transform our responses. Studies on mental health have shown that by giving direction to these primitive emotional languages, we can significantly impact our well-being.

Here are some examples to support sensory intelligence:

- **Pain Triggering Emotion**: Imagine a person who recently experienced a painful breakup. The emotional pain caused by the end of the relationship can linger long after the event has occurred. Every time the person sees a reminder of their ex-partner, memories of the pain resurface, triggering emotions like sadness or even anger. In this case, the pain experienced is not physical but emotional, and it is the mind that keeps replaying and amplifying the hurt, leading to emotional suffering.
- **Pleasure Triggering Emotion:** Consider a student who has been working hard to prepare for an important exam. When the results are announced, and they find out they have performed exceptionally well, the rush of joy, satisfaction, and pride they experience is an emotion triggered by the pleasure of success. The mind's response to this pleasurable event generates emotions, leading to a sense of accomplishment and happiness.
- **Primitive Responses in Modern Context:** A person is walking alone at night when they suddenly hear a loud noise coming from a dark alley. Their heart starts pounding, and a rush of excitement courses through their body. This automatic response of heightened alertness and the readiness to either run away (flight) or confront the threat (fight) is a primitive response to the language of pain. The mind perceives the noise as a potential threat, activating the fight-or-flight response to protect the person from harm.

These examples illustrate how pain and pleasure, whether triggered by the body or the mind, can significantly impact our emotions and well-being. By becoming more self-aware and understanding the role of these languages in our lives, we can take conscious steps to manage our emotions, leading to a healthier and more balanced emotional state.

Let's strive for greater self-awareness, value our sensory intelligence, and navigate our emotions with wisdom and understanding.

Autopilot Mode

Have we ever wondered how we can do things like brushing our teeth or tying our shoelaces without even thinking about it? Well, that's the autopilot mode in action.

Imagine waking up in the morning and going about our day, doing all those familiar things like getting dressed and having breakfast. Our brain has a secret helper inside, guiding us through these routines effortlessly. This clever little helper is our subconscious mind, and it acts as a co-pilot on our journey through life.

But here's the real adventure – our autopilot mode can sometimes be a bit tricky. Our subconscious mind learns from everything we do and experience. It picks up both good and not-so-good stuff along the way. So if we have limiting thoughts or unhelpful habits in our autopilot mode, it might hold us back from fully enjoying life's exciting moments.

But, the best part is that we have the power to train our autopilot mode and make it our greatest ally. We can infuse it with enthusiasm, replace unproductive habits, and transform it into a strength that maintains our focus and efficiency.

It's time to take control, reshape our thoughts, and make each day a thrilling and rewarding ride. Our subconscious mind is our ultimate guide, and together, we'll conquer new horizons with a smile on our face.

Consider some more examples of autopilot mode.

Imagine this: Have we ever been so engrossed in a good book or a fun game that we didn't even notice time passing by? That's autopilot mode in action. When we're so focused and immersed in something, our subconscious mind takes over, and we do things automatically without even thinking about them.

Here's another example: Have we ever zoned out while doing routine tasks like going to market? our mind might have wandered off to daydream or think about something else. That's our autopilot mode at work, making sure we can do these familiar tasks effortlessly.

Let's talk about riding a bike – once we learn how to ride, it becomes almost like second nature. We don't have to think about balancing or pedaling; our subconscious mind takes the wheel, and we cruise along on autopilot mode.

Have we ever noticed how we automatically say "thank you" or "excuse me" when someone does something nice or when we need to get through a crowd? That's autopilot mode helping us use polite manners without even having to think about it.

So, autopilot mode is like having a helpful companion who takes care of routine tasks and lets us focus on the exciting and important stuff. It's a super cool feature of our brains that helps us navigate through life with ease and efficiency. Next time when we find ourselves doing something automatically, we'll know that our amazing subconscious mind is in charge, making our journey through life a fantastic and smooth ride.

Intrapersonal Conflict

In our exciting journey of understanding subliminal storyline, we've come across something fascinating called "intrapersonal conflict." Imagine having different thoughts and feelings, like two little voices inside your head, each with its own ideas. Sometimes these thoughts don't agree, and it can create a sense of discomfort, like being torn between two choices. When our words, actions, and thoughts are not aligned, it creates intrapersonal conflict.

For example, many of us make sure our children are responsible for their studies. This sense is ingrained in our inner self. And, neglecting our own professional responsibilities can lead to internal conflict. In the same manner, the majority of us expect responsible behaviour and good service from the professionals we engage with, reflecting our own inherent values. However, if we're disregarding our own professional responsibilities, it creates an inner conflict within us.

These conflicts might not be easy to notice, but they have detrimental effects on wellbeing.

Another example is when we expect something from others that we don't do ourselves. Let's say we want our friend to be kind and understanding, but sometimes we find it hard to be kind ourselves. This creates conflict because our beliefs and actions don't resonate.

But hold on, there are some tricky consequences of intrapersonal conflict. Feeling uncomfortable inside can make us anxious and stressed. It is very difficult to decide on something while these little voices are arguing. And sometimes, this conflict can affect our relationships with others. We might become defensive or start arguments because we're feeling torn inside. We might resist changing our beliefs or actions, even if it would make us feel better, sticking to old habits, even if they create discomfort.

As we continue our journey through creating awareness about life, the knowledge of intrapersonal conflict becomes vital. By learning to navigate these internal struggles, we can become more self-aware and lead more balanced lives.

Rose grew up in a society that believed in traditional gender roles and expectations. They told her that her purpose in life was to become a devoted wife and mother, putting her family's needs above her own dreams and ambitions.

As Rose grew older, she felt a conflict within herself. She had always been an independent and ambitious woman with her own dreams. She wanted a career, personal fulfillment, and the freedom to pursue her passions. But these desires clashed with the beliefs she was taught as a child.

This inner struggle made Rose feel tormented. She was torn between what society expected of her and what she truly wanted. This conflict created a lot of discomfort and unease in her mind.

The more Rose tried to fit into the expected roles, the worse she felt. She felt trapped and suffocated, always feeling guilty and ashamed for even thinking about her own dreams. The fear of judgment from others made her suffer even more.

The conflict affected her relationships too. Rose couldn't be herself around her family and friends because she was constantly trying to meet their expectations. She felt lonely and empty, unable to pursue her true passions.

Her mental and emotional health suffered too. Rose felt anxious, sad, and trapped in a life that didn't feel right for her. The burden of conflicting beliefs and desires weighed heavily on her, taking away any happiness or self-acceptance.

Sadly, Rose's suffering continued without relief. She faced internal battles every day, torn between what she was told to be and who she really was. This inner conflict made her doubt her worth, and she felt like she couldn't reach her full potential.

In Rose's life, we see the adverse impact of intrapersonal conflict. It's a sad reminder of the pain and struggle that arise when societal expectations clash with personal desires. Rose's story shows how destructive it can be when we deny ourselves the chance to be true to who we are.

Perception Unmasked

> *"Every thought a person dwells upon, whether he expresses it or not, either damages or improves his life."*
>
> ***– Lucy Mallory***

The fascinating world of perception is interesting in how it shapes our view of the world around us. The essence of human life lies in our subjective experience, which is built on our perception. Each one of us has our own unique way of experiencing the world, and this is deeply influenced by how we perceive things around us.

Our perception colours everything we see, feel, and think. It's a superpower that influences our emotions, attitudes, and how we see life itself.

Sometimes we might think the world is a wonderful and friendly place, while other times, we might feel like it's a scary and unfriendly one.

The great thinker Albert Einstein once said, "*The most important decision we make is whether we believe we live in a friendly or hostile universe.*" It's amazing how our beliefs can impact our experiences. When we adopt the idea of a friendly universe, we tend to view things with a more optimistic outlook, and favourable occurrences seem to unfold for us. On the flip side, if we think the universe is hostile, we might feel more cynical and afraid, which can attract more adverse experiences.

But guess what? Our perception is a lens that filters what we see, based on our beliefs, past experiences, and even our biases. Two people can look at the same event and see it completely differently, just like how we might view the same movie but have different opinions about it.

Speaking of movies, have we ever gotten so absorbed in a film that we felt like we were part of the story? Our minds are amazing at this – as we can temporarily blur the line between reality and imagination. We become emotionally connected to the characters and their experiences, laughing with them, crying with them, and feeling what they feel. It's all because of the power of storytelling and how our minds can empathize and emotionally respond to what we see.

This emotional involvement is temporary, though, and we can tell the difference between the movie world and our real lives. But those emotions and memories can stick with us, even after the movie ends.

What's even more incredible is that this same principle can apply to how we perceive information in our everyday lives. Our minds can sometimes mix up what's real and what's not, especially when we encounter information that aligns with our existing beliefs or triggers strong emotions. Our minds have a tendency to look for information that supports what we already think, and we might not notice or ignore anything that doesn't fit.

Emotional content is also like a magnet for our minds – it grabs our attention and can sway our perception. When we come across information that stirs up our feelings, those emotions can affect how we see that information, sometimes even more than our rational thinking.

And let's not forget about the sources of information. Our minds often trust information from credible sources more, but it's not always easy to figure out what's trustworthy, especially with so much information online.

So, it's essential to be aware of how our perception works and how it can shape our understanding of the world. By being mindful of our beliefs, emotions, and the sources of information we encounter, we can navigate through life with a clearer view and make more informed decisions.

The Enigma Unveiled

Having a special key called self-awareness unlocks the treasure of personal growth and understanding, providing deeper insights into ourselves and our emotions. In this transformative journey, we need to create awareness about self-reflection, which is a compass that guides us in exploring our thoughts and feelings. It acts as a map, helping us navigate through our behaviours, strengths, and areas for improvement. Seeking feedback from others is like having helpful guides along the way, showing us perspectives we might have missed. As we venture deeper, we'll uncover the treasures of our emotions and interests, which help us paint a clearer picture of who we truly are.

During this journey, we come across the incredible concept of the child and youth within us. Can we envisage having a part of ourselves that is always curious, open to new experiences, and filled with wonder? It's a hidden treasure chest of innocence and playfulness. We need to recognize nurturing this inner child, to create better understanding in life.

We all have this treasure within us. By acknowledging and validating each other's inner child, we create a beautiful bond of connection. It reminds us to be patient, kind, and forgiving, knowing that we all carry our own unique experiences and fears. Just like how children approach the world with curiosity and excitement, we can approach others with the same sense of wonder and understanding.

The Energy of Youthful Spirit on the other hand is like a spark that ignites a fire. This energy is characterized by enthusiasm, a drive for exploration, and a thirst for adventure. It propels us to accept challenges, seek new experiences, and push boundaries, inspiring personal growth, ambition, and resilience. When we channel this vibrant spirit into productive and fulfilling activities, it brings immense satisfaction.

Now, let's venture deeper into the realms of happiness. Picture having a well-balanced treasure chest, containing both the child and youth within us. The child represents innocence, wonder, and boundless curiosity, while the youth embodies vitality, energy, and a thirst for adventure. Together, these aspects play a crucial role in maintaining a happy and peaceful life.

Connecting with our inner child and youth is a transformative practice that brings us closer to our true selves. It allows us to tap into our creativity, curiosity, and emotional authenticity, fostering more meaningful connections with others. When we acknowledge and nurture our inner child and youth, we create a safe space for vulnerability, empathy, and emotional intimacy to flourish.

However, we notice that males and females might have different treasures within them. Females often shine with the brilliance of their inner child, while males showcase the vibrant energy of their youth. Understanding and appreciating these differences allows us to create a harmonious balance between the two, leading to a fulfilling and joyful existence.

Gender equality doesn't mean ignoring our differences. Instead, it means creating a space where everyone is respected and valued, regardless of their gender.

As we continue to explore the wonders of our inner selves, there are some essential things to remember. In our pursuit of happiness, we must cherish and nurture the child and youth within us.

Although these aspects may not always be readily apparent, they hold significant importance and warrant our attention.

One of the Highly Misunderstood Term "Sexuality"

At its core, sexuality is a rich tapestry of biological, psychological, and sociocultural factors that interplay to shape a person's feelings, attractions, behaviours, and identities. Yet, it extends far beyond the confines of sexual orientation or gender identity, encompassing a vast spectrum of experiences.

To gain a deeper understanding of sexuality, we must approach it with an open mind, free from preconceived notions and stereotypes. Recognizing the diversity of human sexuality enables us to appreciate the intricacies of each individual's experiences and expressions. Respecting their autonomy and agency in expressing their own sexuality is paramount, as it fosters a sense of acceptance and inclusivity.

Though human sexuality encompasses various aspects beyond reproduction and pleasure, these narrow perspectives have been deeply ingrained in society. By challenging these limiting viewpoints, we can broaden our understanding and pave the way for a more accepting environment—one that encompasses the full spectrum of human sexual experiences and identities.

Establishing a healthy connection between genders is of utmost importance. It goes beyond merely acknowledging differences; it involves mutual respect, understanding, and emotional connection. Such a connection can have profound effects on personal growth and relationships. When both genders feel seen, heard, and valued, it lays the foundation for a deeper understanding of each other's experiences.

In this balanced and equitable partnership, traditional gender roles and stereotypes lose their hold. Instead, a collaborative approach to relationships and personal growth emerges, where each individual's unique strengths and qualities are appreciated.

To foster this deeper connection, we must rewrite the scripts in our subconscious minds, challenging societal conditioning that perpetuates harmful gender stereotypes. Adopting a revised connection between genders enables us to navigate relationships with empathy, emotional intelligence, and a broader perspective on life.

By fostering an awareness of the beauty of human sexuality and connections, we step into a more empowered life – one that honors individual journeys and embraces the richness of diversity. In this inclusive environment, we discover the true essence of our interconnectedness as human beings.

Prosperity Equilibrium

In our lives, two distinct aspects are represented by the acronym MPR: Mental health, Physical health, and Relationship health (MPR 1) versus Money, Position, and Resources (MPR 2). Many of us may be unaware or ignorant of this crucial aspect of life, but upon thoughtful examination, we uncover a significant disparity in how we perceive and prioritize them.

MPR 1 comprises the core elements of our well-being: our mental state, physical vitality, and the quality of our relationships. These aspects are vital for our overall wellbeing and fulfillment. On the other hand, MPR 2 encompasses external measures of success, such as financial resources, occupational status, and access to opportunities.

Sadly, our conditioning often places a higher value on MPR 2, leading us to believe that material wealth and societal status are everything. This conditioning starts at a young age and becomes deeply ingrained in our subconscious minds. As a result, we tend to prioritize the pursuit of money, position, and resources while neglecting our mental and physical health and the quality of our relationships.

This imbalance has real-life consequences, as many of the problems in our lives arise from neglecting MPR 1. When we focus solely on MPR 2, we risk compromising our well-being and experiencing feelings of emptiness and dissatisfaction. We may neglect self-care, our mental well-being, and the nurturing of meaningful relationships.

In reality, MPR 2 is meant to support and enhance MPR 1. While money, position, and resources can provide security and opportunities, they should not overshadow our mental health, physical well-being, and relationships.

The balance of these two sets of assets shapes our prosperity. It's important to recognize the difference between them, as this disparity could pose a risk to our overall well-being.

Being aware of the significance of MPR 1 is crucial for nurturing our mental and physical well-being. Never underestimate the value of investing in fostering congenial relationships, as they contribute to greater overall well-being and a deeper sense of contentment. It's time to shift our perspectives towards a more balanced and integrated approach to life—one that values both MPR 1 and MPR 2 in their rightful places.

From a young age, Lal was conditioned to believe that success in money, position, and resources was the key to happiness and fulfillment. Influenced by societal expectations and driven by personal ambition, Lal dedicated his life to achieving great wealth, climbing the corporate ladder, and accumulating material possessions.

As the years went by, Lal's dedication and hard work paid off, and he did indeed achieve remarkable success in terms of the second MPR. He became financially affluent, held a prestigious position in his field, and surrounded himself with opulent luxuries. On the surface, it seemed as though he had it all.

However, despite his external achievements, deep within, Lal felt an incessant void and an overwhelming sense of failure. The pursuit of wealth and social status had consumed him, leaving little room for self-care, personal relationships, and genuine happiness. He constantly felt a gnawing emptiness, a persistent reminder that something vital was missing from his life.

Lal's mental health began to deteriorate as the weight of his achievements bore down on him. The constant pressure to maintain his position and accumulate more wealth led to chronic stress and anxiety, resulting in sleepless nights and constant restlessness. The once-driven and ambitious man now found himself trapped in a never-ending cycle of discontent.

Moreover, Lal's physical health suffered as he neglected his well-being in the relentless pursuit of his ambitions. Long hours at work, an unhealthy lifestyle, and a lack of self-care took a toll on his body. He found himself drained, physically exhausted, and plagued by various health issues. The pursuit of the second MPR had left him depleted and broken.

But perhaps the most significant toll was on Lal's relationships. His relentless focus on wealth and status had alienated his loved ones, leaving him feeling isolated and disconnected. He had lost touch with the meaningful connections he once cherished. He longed for genuine human interaction, but the people around him seemed to be drawn more to his wealth than his true self.

Lal's life is a poignant reminder of the consequences that can arise from an unbalanced fixation on the second MPR. His suffering is a cautionary tale, highlighting the potential pitfalls of prioritizing external markers of success over essential aspects of well-being.

Principle of Repetition

Our subconscious mind holds powerful programs that influence our lives. These programs are shaped by our past experiences, beliefs, and emotions, impacting our thoughts and actions on a subconscious level.

For instance, if we believe we are not good enough, it can lead to self-doubt, influencing our decisions and causing us to avoid opportunities. Similarly, past experiences of abandonment can lead us to behave in ways that push others away, affecting our relationships.

Childhood experiences, emotional intensity, and repetition are key ways our subconscious mind is programmed. Our experiences during childhood can leave a lasting impact, as our brains are sensitive and developing during this time. Experiences like care and support create a strong foundation, while experiences like abuse or neglect can lead to destructive patterns of thought and behaviour.

Emotions are closely linked to our subconscious programming, and intense emotional experiences can create strong associations. For example, a traumatic event can lead to fear-based responses in similar situations.

The good news is that we can reprogram our subconscious mind through various techniques and practices. Repetition is an essential factor in this process. Consistently reinforcing a particular message, thought, or action can create new patterns of thinking and behaviour.

While repetition can be powerful and beneficial, it is essential to focus on constructive practices. Repeating harmful behaviours can have detrimental effects on our well-being and development. Being mindful of what we repeat in our lives can lead to self-growth and personal transformation.

The benefit of repetition lies in its cumulative effect, especially when it comes to creating new subconscious programming. As we repeatedly reinforce a thought or behaviour, it gains strength and becomes increasingly likely to take root as a habit within our subconscious mind.

Our daily practices also play a role in reprogramming our subconscious mind. What we do every day reinforces our subconscious programming and helps create new ways of thinking and behaving. The way we behave sparks the formation of fresh neural connections in our brain, resulting in shifts in our thinking, emotions, and overall actions.

Here are a few more points about the principle of repetition.

- **Enhanced Learning**: Repetition forms the bedrock of effective learning. When we engage in the repeated review of information or practice a skill over and over again, it enhances our ability to recall and perform those tasks effortlessly. This is precisely why repetition is a prevalent technique employed in educational settings, as it helps us better understand new concepts and retain knowledge for the long term.
- **Mastery and Skill Development**: The principle of repetition is essential for achieving mastery in any field. Whether it's sports, music, art, or a professional skill, regular and deliberate practice through

repetition is the key to improving performance and reaching a high level of proficiency.

- **Behavioural Conditioning**: Repetition plays a crucial role in behavioural conditioning. By consistently repeating desired behaviours and rewarding creative actions, we can reinforce and encourage constructive habits. On the other hand, acknowledging and minimizing repetitive limiting patterns can lead to transformative behavioural changes.
- **Building Confidence**: Repeating tasks or challenges and experiencing gradual improvement can boost self-confidence. As we see ourselves making progress through repetition, we gain a sense of accomplishment and belief in our abilities to overcome obstacles.
- **Cultural Transmission**: Repetition is heavily entrenched in the way cultures transfer traditions and practices. Through repetition, customs and rituals are perpetuated and handed down from one generation to another.
- **Creating Impactful Messages**: In communication and advertising, the principle of repetition is employed to create more memorable and impactful messages. Repeating key points or slogans helps ensure the information is retained and understood by the audience.
- **Strengthening Relationships**: In relationships, regular expressions of love, appreciation, and support reinforce the bonds between individuals. Small, repeated acts of kindness can have a significant impact on the quality of a relationship over time.

Suri had a big dream of learning to play the guitar. Every time he heard the beautiful melodies created by the instrument, he was filled with a longing to make music of his own. But there was one problem – Suri had never played any musical instrument before, and he felt unsure if he could ever learn to play the guitar.

Despite his doubts, Suri was determined to give it a try. He knew that learning to play the guitar would not be easy, but he was willing to put in the effort. So, he decided to create a practice plan and schedule to use the principle of repetition to achieve his dream.

Suri got himself a beginner's guitar and set aside time for practice every day. He started with a simple schedule - 30 minutes of practice in the morning. At first, his fingers felt clumsy, and the strings seemed hard to press down. But he didn't give up. Suri knew that repetition was the key to success, so he kept on playing, even if it didn't sound perfect at first.

In his practice plan, Suri focused on mastering the basic chords and finger placements. He would practice each chord individually, repeating them over and over again until he felt comfortable. Then, he would try switching between chords, making sure to do it slowly and accurately.

Every day, Suri would watch tutorial videos to learn new techniques and try to mimic the movements of skilled guitarists. He also used online resources to find simple songs with easy chords to practice. He would play those songs repeatedly, working on getting the rhythm and timing just right.

As the days turned into weeks, Suri noticed a change. His fingers were getting more agile, and he could press the strings with ease. The melodies that once sounded jumbled were now becoming clear and harmonious. Suri was making progress, and it filled him with a sense of accomplishment.

With each passing day, Suri's dedication to learning the guitar grew stronger. He had successfully applied the principle of repetition – by practicing consistently, he was slowly reprogramming his mind and body to master the instrument. It wasn't always easy, and there were times when he felt frustrated or wanted to give up. But Suri reminded himself of his dream and the principle of repetition that had brought him this far.

As the months went by, Suri's guitar playing improved tremendously. He could play his favourite songs with confidence and even started composing some tunes of his own. The guitar had become his companion, and through the principle of repetition and his practice plan, he had turned his dream into a reality.

Suri's journey to learn the guitar with his well-structured practice plan and consistent schedule serves as a beautiful example of how repetition can help us achieve our dreams. With perseverance and dedication, he was able to overcome his initial doubts and transform into a skilled guitarist.

Responsiveness

In today's fast-paced world filled with information, responsiveness is a valuable skill that can greatly impact our decision-making. Being responsive means making timely and effective choices by considering sensibility, sensitivity, and emotion.

Every day, we make many decisions in our lives. We might have heard people say, "I have made decisions on my own." But what does that truly mean? Who is behind those decisions? Most of the time, it's our conditioning or past experiences that influence us to make a decision. It's important to be aware and sensible when making choices.

Let's explore how these elements contribute to enhancing our decision-making abilities and understand their power in helping us respond effectively to various situations.

Sensibility: A Foundation for Responsive Decision-Making

Sensibility serves as the foundation for responsive decision-making. It involves both emotional and intellectual responsiveness. Emotional sensibility allows us to recognize and understand our own emotions, which helps us process information in a holistic way. On the other hand, intellectual sensibility nurtures critical thinking and analytical skills, enabling us to evaluate complex data and extract valuable insights. When we cultivate sensibility, we build a strong base for making decisions that can adapt to changing circumstances.

Sensitivity: Handling Large Data Sets with Precision

Sensitivity is a vital aspect of sensibility, especially when it comes to handling large amounts of data. Being sensitive means having a keen ability to perceive and interpret subtle patterns and nuances within vast information. This skill empowers us to identify relevant details, make connections, extract essential insights from extensive data sets, and navigate through large amounts of information with precision, which in turn facilitates more informed and responsive decision-making.

Addressing Emotional Weaknesses: Unleashing Responsive Potential

To optimize our responsiveness, it is crucial to address any emotional weaknesses that might hinder our decision-making process. Emotional weaknesses like anxiety, impulsivity, or biases can cloud our judgement and lead to less rational choices. Developing emotional intelligence, makes us recognize and regulate our emotions better, thus minimizing the impact of these weaknesses. Through self-awareness, emotional regulation, and strategies to manage biases, we unlock our responsive potential and make decisions based on a balanced integration of reason and emotion.

Being responsive allows us to act promptly and effectively, enabling us to navigate the challenges of life with greater confidence and success.

Joe was known for his kindness and willingness to help others. He had a natural compassion that drew people to him, and he was always ready to lend a helping hand to those in need. However, Joe had a tendency to be emotionally driven, which sometimes caused him to overlook the challenges in his own life and the needs of his own family.

One day, Joe came across a man named Mark who was going through a tough time. Without a second thought, Joe impulsively offered his assistance, focusing solely on the financial aspect of Mark's struggles. He wanted to help Mark find stability and ease his burdens. Little did Joe know, Mark had been handling his difficulties privately and had not sought help from others. Moreover, there were many other individuals in the town facing various hardships beyond financial struggles. Sadly, Joe's fixation on money and his emotional need for financial stability prevented him from seeing the broader range of needs within his community.

As time passed, Joe's emotional vulnerabilities continued to surface. His impulsive nature led him into several situations where he struggled to provide adequate help. This emotional impulsivity sometimes resulted in misunderstandings and strained relationships.

Joe's emotional weaknesses proved to be a challenge for him to manage. While he genuinely cared for others, his actions were not always well thought out, and his efforts to help sometimes fell short. Despite his good intentions, his emotional vulnerability sometimes hindered his ability to make well-balanced decisions.

As the days went by, Joe's emotional growth remained a work in progress. He realized that he needed to find a way to temper his impulses with thoughtfulness and consider the consequences of his actions. However, this was not an easy task for him, and he often struggled with finding the right balance between his emotions and his desire to be helpful.

In the end, Joe's emotional weaknesses, like those in many individuals, were a part of his personality. They made him compassionate and caring but also posed challenges for him and those around him. His life centered around the monetary aspect of life, leaving other important aspects of life aside. His emotional vulnerabilities remained a constant aspect of his life.

Environmental Influencers

The environment isn't just about nature but literally all the things that surround us. It includes many things like information we get, what we watch for fun, how society works, the food we eat, and our practices. It has a profound impact on our overall well-being. One significant factor that affects our mood and emotional state is the food we eat. If we start our day with a wholesome breakfast of fresh fruits and whole grains, we'd likely feel energized and ready to take on the day. Conversely, when we regularly partake in hyperpalatable food, we risk compromising our health.

For example, a teenager constantly exposed to unrealistic beauty standards. This can lead to feelings of inadequacy, body image issues, and a distorted sense of self-worth. The pressure to conform to these standards might result in anxiety and a constant need for validation, impacting their mental health and overall confidence. The pervasive influence of information resources could hinder their ability to develop healthy self-concept and authentic relationships, potentially leading to long-term struggles.

Hence we see that our environment plays a crucial role in terms of stress and vulnerability. Imagine a person living in an underprivileged neighbourhood with limited resources and opportunities. They may face constant stress due to financial struggles, unsafe living conditions, and limited access to healthcare. This ongoing stress can take a toll on their mental health, leading to anxiety and depression.

On the contrary, someone from a supportive and stable environment, surrounded by caring people, may have better tools to cope with stress and handle difficulties. This supportive environment can act as a buffer against mental health challenges, providing them with a sense of safety and emotional security.

Our family and work environments are significant contributors to our mental well-being. Think about a person with a loving and understanding family. They have open communication, and their emotions are acknowledged and validated. This supportive family environment helps them feel secure, accepted, and emotionally stable.

However, envision someone dealing with toxic family dynamics, where conflicts and misunderstandings are prevalent. This toxic environment can lead to feelings of anxiety, isolation, and low self-esteem, impacting their mental health and overall happiness.

Similarly, the work environment can greatly influence our mental well-being. An individual working in a supportive workplace with understanding colleagues will likely experience job satisfaction. On the other hand, someone in a toxic work environment, with constant pressure, unrealistic expectations, and unsupportive colleagues, may experience burnout and chronic stress.

Epigenetics, an exciting field of study, helps us understand the interplay between our genes and the environment. Let's consider two people with similar genetic backgrounds. One person grows up in a nurturing and caring environment, with access to good education and support. The other person grows up in a challenging environment, facing adversity and limited resources.

Epigenetics reveals that these different environments can affect how the same genes are expressed, leading to different outcomes in terms of physical and mental health. The person in the supportive environment might have a lower risk of mental health issues, while the other person may be more susceptible to stress-related problems.

Individuals grappling with low self-esteem tend to possess a heightened susceptibility to the impact of external influences. In their case, the environment plays a pivotal role in exacerbating their existing challenges. The presence of low self-esteem makes them more receptive to the cues, judgments, and expectations originating from their surroundings. Consequently, these environmental inputs have the potential to amplify their internal emotional conflicts. Such influences function as a catalyst, intensifying their pre-existing feelings of inadequacy.

Nemi, a promising engineer in a quaint town, set out on a journey filled with dreams and aspirations. One day, she met a remarkable man whom she chose as her life partner. They were deeply in love and decided to start their journey together.

As Nemi pursued her professional career, she faced numerous challenges and responsibilities that brought immense stress into her life. However, she didn't realize the impact of her work environment on her well-being. She tried to handle everything on her own, unaware of the consequences that awaited her.

A year later, Nemi and her husband welcomed their first child into the world. They were filled with joy and excitement, looking forward to the adventures of parenthood. However, their happiness quickly turned to despair as they discovered that their little one was facing health difficulties. They were devastated and determined to find answers.

Day after day, they consulted countless doctors and underwent painful surgeries to help their child. Each passing moment was filled with anxiety, fear, and an overwhelming longing for a solution. They sought experts and conducted numerous tests, hoping to understand the cause of their child's health issues. Following a series of genetic tests, the results indicated the absence of any genetic issues.

Despite their efforts, the results brought no clarity, leaving Nemi and her husband feeling lost and bewildered. They couldn't understand why their child was suffering, and it weighed heavily on them.

A few years later, their second child was born with no health difficulties, bringing a moment of wondrous joy to Nemi and her husband. They celebrated the arrival of their healthy baby. Interestingly, this occurred as a complete coincidence since they hadn't made any significant changes to their lifestyles since their firstborn. However, there was a shift in the atmosphere in her home and professional life when the second baby was conceived.

Nemi's story serves as a poignant reminder of the consequences that can arise from unawareness and ignorance. It underscores the tremendous toll on a couple's emotional, financial, and personal well-being when environmental influencers are not considered. Her journey stands as a call to action, urging others to seek knowledge and value awareness to minimize the costs that can arise from overlooking the significant impact of our environment on our lives.

As we journey through life, it becomes evident that many people remain unaware of the profound impact of environmental influencers until they face hardships or challenging circumstances. It is disheartening to witness this prevailing pattern of ignorance, where individuals continue living in the same manner, unknowingly creating similar challenges into their lives again and again. The missed opportunities for growth and the unnecessary suffering caused by this lack of awareness evoke a sense of sorrow.

One particularly concerning trend is observed among young individuals. They often live in the present, buoyed by the resilience of their biology during their formative years, without considering the long-term consequences of their actions. Unaware of how their current lifestyle choices can shape their overall well-being, they navigate through life with a sense of invincibility. But when they eventually face difficulties resulting from their present habits and choices, there's a troubling tendency to deflect responsibility and blame external factors, failing to recognize the role their own lifestyle played in shaping their circumstances. This disconnection from their past actions perpetuates a cycle of ignorance and missed opportunities for personal growth.

To break free from this cycle, it is crucial to instill a sense of self-awareness in young individuals. Encouraging them to take ownership of their life and fostering a culture of self-reflection and accountability empowers them to make meaningful changes and create a healthier life. By acknowledging the power they hold in shaping their own lives, they can move towards personal responsibility and growth.

Awareness allows us to recognize the potential long-term consequences of our actions and empowers us to create a more supportive and nurturing environment for ourselves.

Chapter 3

UNMASKING THE IDENTITY

"Knowing ourselves is the beginning of all wisdom."

– Aristotle

Let's join hands on a transformative journey of self-discovery, where we will unmask our true identity hidden beneath the layers of conditioning and societal influences. In this quest, we will delve deep into our core being, beyond the external pressures that often obscure our authentic selves, like a shining light covered by clouds. Our inner childlike wonder and youthful spirit may have been suppressed but we hold the key to unlocking our true essence.

Whenever we immerse ourselves in the imaginary world of movies and stories, we discover profound insights into our true selves through the characters portrayed within them. These experiences have the ability to awaken dormant aspects of our identity, reminding us of the pure and unaltered essence within us. As we move on this introspective journey, we will imbibe the messages conveyed through these mediums, allowing them to touch our inner self. With each revelation, we will reconnect with the child and youth that still live within us, eager to be set free. Our authentic selves will emerge, shining brightly like the stars in the night sky.

Through this process of self-awareness, we will rediscover the beauty of our true nature. So, let us take this adventure hand in hand, uncovering the magnificent identity that lies within us. Together, we will unfold the wonders of who we are, unmasking the essence of our being with joy and wonderment.

Let's explore it through a collection of anecdotes.

#1

In a bustling neighbourhood, a young toy seller caught the attention of a homeowner as he admired the owner's magnificent house. The compassionate homeowner offered the boy a chance to step inside the house, which filled the boy with delight. As he explored the interior, he couldn't help but inquire about the price of such a splendid house. The homeowner replied that he didn't know because it was a gift from his parents. This response made the boy pause and reflect. When the homeowner asked if he also expected a grand gift from his parents, the boy instead replied that he wished to present a similar gift to his parents.

Analysis: We appreciate this toy seller boy who highlights the inherent desires of kindness and empathy within our subconscious minds. These qualities, deeply rooted in humanity, have the power to bring people together, foster caring relationships, and create a sense of unity and harmony.

#2

In a quiet village, there lived a couple who dedicated their lives to raising their child. However, as their child grew older, they faced constant disrespect and rejection. Despite their efforts to connect, their child continued to distance themselves, leaving the couple sad and feeling unappreciated. They grappled with the pain of being rejected by their own child, longing for a bond that seemed unattainable.

Analysis: The story of the disrespected parents highlights the deep-seated subconscious understanding of the love, regard and care we inherently have for our parents. It evokes a disapproval for the child's behaviour, emphasising the significance of the parent-child bond and the subconscious desire for harmonious and respectful relationships within the family unit.

#3

In a small town, a mischievous dog named Buster found himself in a series of hilarious escapades. From stealing socks and hiding them in unexpected places to chasing his own tail in circles, Buster left everyone in stitches. His antics brought joy and laughter to the neighbourhood, turning even the gloomiest of days into moments of pure comedy. No one could resist the infectious laughter that followed Buster wherever he went, making him the beloved comedian of the town.

Analysis: Here Buster leaves a good impression due to its hilarious acts. When we engage in reading a humorous story or watching a comedy scene, our inner joy and liking are often reflected. These moments tap into our subconscious mind, allowing our true sense of humour and joy to emerge. Oftentimes, our conditioning can suppress or overlook our innate happiness. These experiences remind us of the importance of embracing our inner joy and finding opportunities to let it shine, allowing us to live a more authentic and fulfilling life.

#4

Two friends, Jack and Tom, were on a thrilling road trip, filled with laughter and unforgettable memories. They shared a deep bond and trusted each other completely. However, as they journeyed further, Jack's true colours began to surface. In a moment of greed, he betrayed Tom, leaving him stranded in a remote location. Tom was devastated by this unexpected turn of events, realising that their friendship had been built on false pretenses. It was a painful moment for Tom from a trusted and reliable friend Jack.

Analysis: The story of Jack's betrayal reflects our subconscious aversion to acts of betrayal and rejection. It reveals our inherent dislike for actions that go against trust, loyalty, and integrity. The subconscious mind instinctively recognizes the importance of maintaining genuine connections and being true to our commitments. It reinforces the notion that betrayal and deceit are contrary to the values we hold dear, leading to feelings of disappointment and a deep-seated resistance towards such behaviour.

#5

In a small, forgotten town, nestled amidst rolling hills and whispering trees, a young girl named Lily discovered a secret that shattered her. Behind the facade of a seemingly ordinary farmhouse lay a sinister truth—a cruel and twisted world where animals were subjected to unspeakable horrors. Determined to expose the darkness and be their voice, Lily courageously rallied a group of kind-hearted people who, united by compassion, vowed to dismantle the shadows of animal cruelty and restore hope to those who had suffered in silence. With unwavering resolve, they started a mission to bring justice to the voiceless, illuminating the power of empathy and proving that even the smallest acts of kindness can ignite a beacon of change in the darkest of places.

Analysis: The stories of animal cruelty reveal a truth hidden deep within our subconscious minds. As we watch or read these narratives, our innate compassion resurfaces, challenging the conditioning that allows for such cruelty. They awaken our moral compass and inspire us to align our actions with the empathy we inherently possess.

#6

In a small café nestled on a bustling street, the sound of laughter and conversation danced through the air. Amidst the lively chatter, a solitary figure sat hunched over a steaming cup of coffee, lost in thought. The café walls hummed with the gentle strumming of a guitar, and the haunting voice of a singer filled the room. As the melodies weaved through the air, a remarkable transformation unfolded. The figure's gaze softened, and a smile graced the face. It was as if the music had reached deep into the core, unlocking a floodgate of emotions. Memories surged forth, evoking moments of joy, love, and even melancholy. The power of music became evident, transcending the boundaries of time and space.

Analysis: Music speaks a language beyond words, connecting the figure to a larger human experience. In that very moment, amidst the rhythmic tapestry of sound, the figure realised why people were so drawn to music. It is the universal language that could touch the deepest parts of our being, offering solace, inspiration, and a sense of belonging. It is evident that in the realm of our subconscious minds, music holds a special place. It is like a hidden script, woven intricately into our being. When the first notes of a familiar melody reach our ears, a symphony of emotions awakens within us. Memories long forgotten resurface, carrying us to different times and places. The rhythm taps into our primal instincts, stirring our bodies to move, to dance. The lyrics speak to the depths of our inner self, echoing the unspoken thoughts and desires we often keep hidden. Music becomes the language through which our subconscious communicates, expressing what words alone cannot convey. It is a sacred script written within us, a language that transcends boundaries and unites us all.

#7

In a bustling city park, a street musician perched on a weathered bench, his guitar strings resonating with heartfelt melodies. As people strolled by, their eyes fixed on their destinations, a young woman caught sight of the musician. Intrigued, she paused for a moment, her feet tapping in synchrony with the rhythm. Unbeknownst to anyone around her, a symphony of movement unfolded within her core. With a subtle sway of her hips and a gentle nod of her head, she embraced the dance that stirred inside. It was an unspoken language, an intimate conversation between her inner rhythm and the musician's melodies. In that transcendent moment, the world melted away, and she danced engrossed in her own private reverie. Passersby glanced at her curiously, but her spirit remained undeterred. For in the depths of her being, she knew that dancing wasn't confined to grand stages or polished ballrooms—it was an expression of the raw, untamed energy within. With every step, she reclaimed her joy, her freedom, and a connection to the universal pulse that beats within every human being.

Analysis: The enjoyment and resonance experienced by individuals as they witness the young lady's dance provide insights into the presence of dance within their subconscious minds. When observing her graceful movements and infectious rhythm, a connection is formed on a deeper level. It is as if the dance strikes a chord within them, eliciting a profound response. This response signifies that dance is not only a physical act but also an inherent part of human nature. The subconscious mind, hidden beneath the layers of conscious thought, holds the script of our deepest desires and inclinations. Through the enjoyment of the young lady's dance, individuals tap into this subconscious script, unlocking a part of themselves that is attuned to movement and expression. The joy experienced serves as confirmation that dance resonates at a fundamental level, transcending cultural and societal boundaries. It reminds us that dance is not limited to trained professionals or formal settings but is an inherent part of the human experience. Thus, the enjoyment of the young lady's dance serves as a testament to the presence of dance within our subconscious minds, inviting us to the innate joy of movement and the power of self-expression.

#8

Two friends, Bob and Remi, were very close. They both graduated from the same college. Bob always felt a sense of pride for Remi and held good wishes for him, recognizing his immense talent. However, when Remi secured a good job, Bob unexpectedly experienced a subtle form of jealousy. This internal conflict came as a profound shock to Bob, as he discovered an unanticipated aspect of himself.

Analysis: The story above highlights how even in close friendships, subtle forms of jealousy can arise. This is a product of an ignorant mind. Bob's unexpected experience of jealousy towards Remi, despite their strong bond, serves as a reminder of the hidden truth of human emotions. It underscores the potential harm that envy can inflict on personal well-being, as it disrupts the dynamics within relationships and clouds one's own path to contentment.

These anecdotes help us understand our subconscious mind and discover our true selves. When we dive into more of these stories, we get to know how our minds work in amazing ways.

For example, have we ever spent peaceful moments in nature, feeling a strong connection to the world around us? It's a special feeling of calmness inside. Sometimes, we possess an innate understanding without a clear reason, harboring our own reservoir of wisdom within us.

As mentioned earlier, we can experience similar revelations about ourselves while watching movies. Being creative, like drawing or writing stories, is awesome too. It's a way to express ourselves and uncover our true selves. Did we know that our childhood memories shape who we are today - our beliefs, interests, and even our fears come from those memories?

Let's listen to the whispers of our subconscious, allow our true essence to shine, and live in harmony with the script that defines us. It's an adventure that will lead us to a deeper understanding of ourselves at our very core.

Chapter 4

MOR- MODEL OF RESPONSIBILITY

"Nothing was ever achieved without perseverance"

– *Jim Valvano*

This powerful tool encourages us to prioritize responsibility over rights when shaping our lives. When we take ownership of our actions and decisions, this leads us to a path of peace and happiness – something we all desire. Throughout this exploration, we will uncover the essence of MoR: recognizing our responsibilities in life.

Responsibility is a fundamental aspect of human life. It teaches us that we are accountable for our actions and their consequences. Although it may appear challenging at times, taking responsibility is an essential aspect to be ingrained within ourselves. It empowers us to be mindful of our behaviour and consider how our actions impact others. The model of responsibility serves as our guide, helping us to make choices and benefit ourselves.

Taking responsibility for our actions and decisions, helps us learn from our mistakes and gain the skills to make better choices. Along this path, we develop self-awareness and self-control, which are crucial for our growth and well-being.

Taking 100% ownership of our responsibilities is a significant aspect of personal responsibility. It means acknowledging and accepting the tasks that come with our roles and actively fulfilling them with reliability and accountability.

As we progress, we'll also explore the importance of not neglecting our own responsibilities while taking on those which come from outside. Balancing our responsibilities allows us to lead a fulfilling life.

If we neglect our own development, we can't make a meaningful contribution to others' lives. Self-development and having a good self-esteem are essential to take on the responsibilities assigned to us.

As we continue our exploration of the Model of Responsibility (MoR), let's take a closer look at the four categories of responsibilities that shape our lives:

Embracing Responsibility Towards Ourselves

The idea of responsibility revolves around being aware of our duty to ourselves. Personal growth and self-development are vital aspects that apply to everyone. We need to create awareness about taking ownership of our actions and choices, aligning them with our values, and working towards our goals are essential in life. Complete ownership means acknowledging our strengths and weaknesses, and making the best use of our time for self-improvement. We need to cultivate such a mindset to become accountable for the outcomes we create and refrain from blaming external factors for our circumstances. This awareness empowers us to overcome challenges, learn from mistakes, and make conscious decisions that lead to a fulfilling life.

Owning our lives 100% is essential to align with the purpose of life; there's no room for 99 or 99.5%. Taking complete ownership means acknowledging that we are in control of our choices and actions, that we hold the power to shape our lives and this empowers us to lead more fulfilling lives.

Allotted Responsibilities By the Virtue of Situation

These responsibilities are directly related to the roles or positions we find ourselves in different situations. In our professional lives, our job titles determine specific tasks and duties assigned to us. For example, a manager may have responsibilities for overseeing a team, while an accountant may be responsible for handling financial matters. Similarly, in our family settings, different family members may have unique responsibilities based on factors like age, gender, or abilities. For instance, parents may have responsibilities related to household management and providing for the family.

Having clear definitions of these responsibilities is vital for effective discharge. When responsibilities are well-defined, individuals understand what is expected of them, and they can prioritize their tasks accordingly. This clarity promotes a sense of accountability, helping us to fulfill our duties in a timely and effective manner.

Allotted Responsibilities By the Virtue of Delegation

Delegation is all about tasks or duties assigned to us by others that trust us with specific responsibilities. This happens in different areas of life, like at work or in personal relationships. In the workplace, managers delegate tasks to team members based on their skills. And in a relationship, partners may delegate household chores or financial responsibilities based on their strengths and preferences.

When we accept a delegated task, it becomes an allotted responsibility for us. This means that we are accountable for completing the task to the best of our ability and within the given timeframe. Effective communication with the delegator is crucial to ensure progress and address any questions or concerns that may arise during the task's completion. By taking ownership of the delegated responsibility and communicating effectively, we build trust and maintain a harmonious working relationship. The awareness about such responsibility is vital.

Allotted Responsibilities By the Virtue of a Sudden Happening

Life can sometimes present us with unexpected events or situations that require us to take on new responsibilities. These occurrences can range from sudden illnesses, accidents or some other unexpected happening within our families to unforeseen changes in our communities. In such times, we may find ourselves taking on new roles and duties to support those in need.

While these unforeseen responsibilities can be challenging, they also offer opportunities for personal growth and development. They allow us to discover our adaptability, and they often deepen our sense of understanding. However, managing these responsibilities requires effective time management, communication, and collaboration with others. It's important to strike a balance between fulfilling our new responsibilities and taking care of our existing commitments. Many of us lack awareness about this particular type of responsibility. It's crucial to recognize and understand the importance of this category of responsibility.

In situations where unexpected events may occur, preparation is essential. Just as defense forces prepare for war in times of peace, having emergency plans in place can help us respond swiftly and efficiently to unforeseen circumstances.

Understanding these different categories of responsibilities empower us to lead lives of purpose and impact. When we are aware of the duties and obligations we have towards ourselves, others, and the environment, we become more accountable for our choices and behaviour. This sense of ownership is a powerful tool that provides us with clarity and purpose in our endeavors. It encourages us to make conscious decisions, be proactive in pursuing our goals, and take responsibility for the outcomes.

At this point, it's really important to understand the difference between ownership and possessiveness. Ownership means taking responsibility and feeling like we can make good choices and take care of things that belong to us. When we embrace our roles and duties, it makes us feel free and happy.

But possessiveness is a different story. It comes from fear and makes us feel trapped and bitter. When we're possessive, we cling tightly to things and people, not wanting to let them go.

Knowing this difference can help us have better relationships with ourselves and others, and it also affects how we interact with the world around us. So, it's a pretty big deal to recognize these feelings and act accordingly.

We need to understand another important thing about ownership. Nowadays, technology has made the world super-fast. It's doing amazing things that were once unimaginable, like Artificial intelligence, Quantum computing, Hyperloop, Internet technology, Cloud computing, Space missions, Health tech, Biotechnology, Extended reality, Gigital twin technology and many more.

Everything is changing so quickly around us. But the problem is, many of us are not keeping up with the pace because of lack of ownership in their lives. This leads to them falling behind in their thinking and actions creating a delay in their life. While things are moving fast, people are moving slow, and that creates a lot of problems. It leads to disharmony and causes health issues, both mental and physical, and it affects relationships too.

Hence, it is essential to create awareness about the ownership towards ourselves and of our allotted responsibilities, whether by situation, delegation, or sudden happenings to align ourselves with the purpose of life.

CHAPTER 5

HAPPINESS EXPOSED

"A happy life consists in tranquility of mind."

– Cicero

I want to share something really nice about happiness. It's not just for a special group of people; it's for everyone, no matter what life throws our way.

Happiness is a feeling that everyone can experience. We all have the ability to be happy inside us. But sometimes, we may not even realize what's stopping us from feeling happy. It could be limiting thoughts, beliefs that hold us back, or bad habits we can't shake off.

The people who discover true happiness are the ones who are willing to understand their inner thoughts and feelings. They are aware of the activities of their subconscious mind, which is an automatic pilot that guides our actions without us even knowing. Through this awareness they can break free from the things that stop them from being happy.

To find this joy, it takes effort. We need to figure out what's causing our unhappiness and work on fixing it, clearing the roadblocks that stand in the way of our happiness.

When we consciously choose to have progressive thoughts and act in line with our true selves, happiness starts to fill our lives. We grow and become better versions of ourselves. It's a journey of self-discovery and improvement.

It's the people who actively learn about and use the power of the subconscious mind that find real happiness. They take steps to remove the obstacles in their way and open themselves up to the joy and fulfillment life can offer.

Bindu's warm smile and compassion endeared her to everyone around her. But despite her seemingly contented exterior, Bindu yearned for something deeper in her life – she longed to find true happiness.

In the same town, Bindu witnessed the struggles of her fellow villagers, who often sought solace in fleeting pleasures and material possessions. However, Bindu firmly believed that genuine happiness was not dependent on external factors; rather, it emanated from an internal state of being. She had read about the incredible power of the subconscious mind and how understanding and harnessing it could lead to a life of fulfillment.

She learned about a woman named Meti who had grown up in the same village. Meti had always believed that her worth was tied to her financial success and societal status. Despite accumulating wealth, Meti felt a constant emptiness and lack of fulfillment. Bindu's observations of Meti's life served as a poignant real-life example of the principles she was studying.

Armed with this newfound knowledge, Bindu made a steadfast commitment to remove these hurdles from her own life. She immersed herself in wisdom literature, seeking to gain a deeper understanding of the workings of the subconscious mind. Through her studies, Bindu realized that constraining thoughts, limiting beliefs, and unhealthy patterns of behaviour were the very obstacles that stood in the way of experiencing true happiness.

She delved into deep self-reflection, analyzing her thoughts and actions, with a determined effort to align them with her innermost desires and the script of her subconscious mind. This journey was not without its challenges, for Bindu had to confront her fears, insecurities, and past traumas. But her determination to create a space for happiness to flourish kept her moving forward.

Every day, Bindu practiced self-reflection, visualization, and affirmations to reprogram her subconscious mind. She focused on cultivating creative habits, nurturing personal growth, and filling her with gratitude and kindness. Through these deliberate actions, she gradually cleared the path to her happiness, one step at a time.

As Bindu continued on her journey, her newfound awareness started to have a ripple effect on the lives of those around her. She shared her wisdom and experiences with her fellow villagers, gently guiding them on their paths to happiness. Bindu encouraged them to self-reflect, challenge their limiting beliefs, and take intentional action to remove the obstacles that hindered their own happiness.

Bindu came to realize that happiness was not merely a destination to reach, but rather an ongoing and evolving journey. It was a beautiful process of self-discovery, growth, and intentional living. Bindu had unlocked the key to true happiness, not just for herself but for an entire village.

There's a secret to finding happiness, and it's not as hard as we might think. All we need to do is become more aware of ourselves, understand how our minds work, and take action to make ourselves happy, going on a fun adventure of self-discovery and growth.

No matter where we come from or who we are, happiness is something we can all have. We just need to believe in ourselves and take corresponding steps to align our thoughts and actions with what makes us truly happy.

CHAPTER 6

THE LOW HANGING FRUIT

"Wisdom begins in wonder."

– Socrates

Imagine the owner of a warehouse, who is uncertain about the number of products available in his inventory. Without this essential information, he would struggle to plan and execute successful business deals. Such uncertainty would significantly impact his entire operation, leading to inefficiencies and potential losses. In the business world, knowing the inventory position in various segments is of vital importance for maintaining proper storage, ensuring care for the products, and establishing accountability.

Now, let's draw parallels to our own lives. Our existence is akin to a vast warehouse, filled with a plethora of precious inventories. These invaluable assets represent various natural abilities and life support that we receive from the outside world. We are introduced to these valuable aspects during our formal education, but as time goes on, we often forget to acknowledge their significance and fail to recognize their presence.

These precious inventories are the backbone that supports our lives. When we face challenges and obstacles, they act as powerful tools that can be wielded with wisdom and strength, turning us into formidable warriors ready to conquer any adversity. They provide us with determination.

These are the *Low hanging fruit in the garden of life*. We have abundance of blessings in our lives, but we don't notice them because they seem common and easy to get. But if we start appreciating these blessings, it can bring us lasting happiness. Imagine waking up every morning in a cozy little house, surrounded by near ones, and having a delicious breakfast waiting for us. The sun is shining, and we can hear the birds chirping outside our window. All these wonderful blessings are right there, but sometimes, we tend to overlook them because they've become so familiar and part of our everyday life.

But what if I say that acknowledging and appreciating these blessings can lead us to lasting happiness? It's true. When we cultivate a mindset of gratitude and learn to cherish the simple joys in life, we unlock a source of happiness that transcends fleeting circumstances.

Regrettably, numerous individuals suffer from "Appreciation Deficiency" without even being aware of it. This deficiency acts like a blindfold, obstructing their ability to see the abundance of life. They find it difficult to acknowledge and show gratitude for themselves, others, and their situations. Consequently, those who suffer from this appreciation deficiency often exhibit a victim mentality.

This condition can manifest as a self-loathing mindset, where individuals constantly focus on what's lacking or wrong in their lives. They might find themselves caught in a loop of dissatisfaction and frustration, leading to lower self-esteem to tackle life's challenges. It can also strain their relationships with others.

Moreover, appreciation deficiency can create a never-ending desire for more, making it hard for individuals to be content with what they already have. They might constantly chase after bigger achievements, possessions, or experiences without taking the time to acknowledge and be grateful for the blessings they already possess.

Picture a person always striving for the next promotion or a fancier car without truly appreciating their current job or vehicle. This constant dissatisfaction can leave them feeling unfulfilled, even when they achieve their goals or acquire material possessions.

Appreciation deficiency can also lead to a lack of present-moment awareness. When individuals can't appreciate the beauty of the present moment, they may feel disconnected from life, leading to feelings of emptiness or a lack of fulfillment.

Additionally, this condition can have a profound impact on mental health. Constantly focusing on dissatisfaction can increase stress levels, triggering a cycle of condemning thoughts and emotions. Over time, this can lead to chronic stress, anxiety, and even depression, further affecting an individual's overall well-being.

Krish, a remarkably talented photographer, harbored a concealed struggle – he battled with something known as "Appreciation Deficiency." Behind the lens, his gifted eye captured moments of beauty that seemed to unfold effortlessly. Yet, paradoxically, he couldn't discern the magnificence in his own creations. Rather than embracing the inherent artistry in his work, he scrutinized his photographs, honing in on perceived flaws. This self-critical lens cast shadows on his abilities, causing him to question himself and grow discontented with his artistry.

Even when accolades poured in and admirers lauded Krish's talent and artistic insight, his own self-doubt acted as an impenetrable barrier. He dismissed their praise as mere politeness, incapable of accepting that they genuinely meant it. The authentic appreciation and admiration others held for his work remained shrouded in his skepticism.

As days turned into months, Krish's struggle with appreciation deficiency began to take its toll. The brilliance that once illuminated his creative spirit dimmed, replaced by a cloud of frustration and despondency. Doubts crept in, whispering that he might not truly be a skilled artist, and that his photographs were merely ordinary.

Krish's lack of self-appreciation cast a long shadow over his photography. His pictures, which once radiated with life and passion, now seemed lackluster and uninspired. The vivid colours that once danced harmoniously within his compositions transformed into a monotonous palette.

Regrettably, the weight of his self-doubt became too overwhelming to bear. In a heartrending turn of events, Krish made the painful decision to quit photography entirely. The once-promising trajectory of his photography career came to a sudden halt, leaving behind a sense of aimlessness and unfulfillment. The repercussions of his appreciation deficiency had robbed Krish of the profound joy and unwavering passion that his extraordinary talent could have bestowed upon him.

Krish's story serves as a cautionary tale. It shows us how important it is to recognize and celebrate our own achievements and talents. When we don't appreciate ourselves, it can have serious consequences, taking away the happiness and success we deserve.

We need to be aware of ourselves and our accomplishments. We should not doubt our worth and the value we create in the world.

Now we realize the secret to sustainable happiness. It all starts with appreciation – being grateful for all the good things in our lives.

Sustainable happiness doesn't depend on outside things or rare occasions. It's about finding joy and fulfillment in the present moment.

When we become aware and present, we can remove the barriers that keep us from happiness. We reach out and grab those Low hanging fruit of happiness that are already within our grasp. They stand as precious treasures in the garden of life.

As we gaze upon the garden of life, we marvel at its beauty adorned with an abundance of Low hanging fruit, symbolizing the countless opportunities and blessings within our reach. Let us seize these moments and immerse ourselves fully in the rich experiences that life has to offer with an open mind.

Appreciating the following bountiful array of easily attainable opportunities that bring joy and fulfillment to our lives is essential.

Mental Abilities

Mental abilities are the diverse and remarkable powers of our mind that enable us to navigate through life's challenges and opportunities. They allow us to learn, adapt, and make decisions, making us uniquely human. We need to nurture awareness of these inherent mental capabilities

- **Memory:** Ability to recall information from the past.
- **Attention:** Ability to be fully present, focus on a specific task or conversation without getting distracted.
- **Alertness:** The state of being cautious of potential threats.
- **Problem-Solving:** Skill to find solutions to challenges and puzzles.
- **Critical Thinking:** Analyzing information, questioning ideas, and making informed decisions.
- **Creativity:** Thinking outside the box and coming up with innovative ideas.
- **Logical Reasoning:** Thinking logically and making sense of things.
- **Spatial Reasoning:** Understanding and manipulating visual information mentally.
- **Numerical Skills:** Understanding and working with numbers
- **Emotional Intelligence:** Understanding and managing emotions, both of self and of others.

- **Learning Ability:** Capacity to acquire new knowledge and skills.
- **Adaptability:** Ability to adjust and thrive in different situations.
- **Decision Making:** Skill to choose the best option from different alternatives.
- **Imagination:** Power to create vivid mental images and ideas.
- **Analytical Thinking:** Breaking down complex problems into smaller parts for easier understanding.
- **Communication Skills:** Ability to express oneself effectively and understand others.
- **Time Management:** Skill to set priorities and plan efficiently to make the most of time.
- **Resilience:** Ability to bounce back from setbacks and challenges.
- **Intuition:** Gut feeling or instinct that guides decision-making.

Physical Abilities

Physical abilities encompass a diverse range of incredible attributes that our bodies possess, enabling us to experience and interact with the world around us. These physical abilities create a magnificent symphony that shapes our experiences, enriches our lives, and allows us to cherish the wonders of the world. Awareness of our physical abilities is a must in the process of life.

- **Vision:** The ability to see and perceive the world through our eyes.
- **Smell:** The capacity to detect and identify different scents using our nose.
- **Hear:** The sense of hearing that allows us to perceive sounds.
- **Taste:** The ability to distinguish various flavours using our tongue.
- **Touch:** The sense of touch that enables us to feel textures and sensations.
- **Movement:** The capability to move and control our body.

- **Sweat:** The body's natural way of cooling down through perspiration.
- **Digestion:** The process of breaking down food and absorbing nutrients in our body.
- **Balance:** The ability to maintain stability and stay upright.
- **Flexibility:** The range of motion and suppleness of our muscles and joints.
- **Strength:** The power and capacity of our muscles to exert force.
- **Coordination:** The skill to combine different body movements smoothly and efficiently.
- **Agility:** The ability to move quickly and change direction easily.
- **Reflexes:** Automatic and quick responses to stimuli without conscious thought.
- **Endurance:** The ability to sustain physical activity for extended periods.
- **Speech:** The capability to articulate and produce sounds for communication.
- **Posture:** The way we hold and align our body in different positions.

Body Systems

Body systems are complex webs of organs, tissues, and cells that cooperate harmoniously to carry out crucial functions necessary for our survival and well-being. Each system plays a vital role in keeping the body balanced and functioning optimally. We owe our profound gratitude to the scientific community for unveiling the intricate details of these remarkable systems within our bodies. Their interconnectedness diligently upholds our health, empowering us to engage in daily activities.

- **Respiratory System:** Includes the lungs and airways, responsible for breathing.

- **Cardiovascular System:** Consists of the heart and blood vessels that transport blood and nutrients throughout the body.
- **Digestive System:** Consists of organs like the stomach, intestines, and liver, responsible for digestion and absorption of nutrients.
- **Skeletal System:** Provides support, protection, and movement through bones, joints, and muscles.
- **Immune System:** Defends against infections and diseases, safeguarding the body from harmful invaders.
- **Nervous System:** Includes the brain, spinal cord and nerves, controlling body functions and facilitating communication.
- **Endocrine System:** Regulates bodily processes using hormones secreted by glands like the pituitary, thyroid, and adrenal glands.
- **Muscular System:** Consists of muscles throughout the body that enable movement and provide stability.
- **Integumentary System:** Includes the skin, hair, and nails, protecting the body from external elements and regulating temperature.
- **Lymphatic System:** Comprising lymph nodes, vessels, and lymph, it helps in immune response and the removal of waste from tissues.
- **Reproductive System:** Responsible for reproduction, with different systems in males and females for producing and nurturing offspring.
- **Urinary System:** Consists of the kidneys, ureters, bladder, and urethra, responsible for filtering and removing waste products from the blood through urine.
- **Excretory System:** Includes various organs and structures that eliminate waste products from the body.

Support of People

People power plays a crucial role in our lives right from childhood and continues throughout our journey. The collective support and influence of these individuals enrich our lives and shape our identity. Their encouragement, understanding, and presence offer a sense of joyful shared experiences.

- **Parents:** Our parents are our first and most influential supporters. They provide care, and guidance, laying the foundation for our values and beliefs.
- **Siblings:** Siblings are our lifelong companions and often our first friends. They teach us about sharing, cooperation, and companionship.
- **Close Relatives:** Relatives offer a sense of belonging and extended support. They create a strong sense of family and are there for us during both joyous and challenging times.
- **Close Acquaintances:** These friends become like family, providing emotional support and understanding in various situations.
- **Classmates:** In school, classmates contribute to our learning experience. They offer companionship, help us understand different perspectives, and teach us valuable social skills.
- **Neighbours:** Neighbours create a sense of community and can be a source of support, friendship, and safety.
- **Workplace Acquaintances:** Colleagues and coworkers help us in our professional journey. They share knowledge, expertise, and teamwork, making our work life more fulfilling.
- **Social Companions:** People we interact with in social groups or organizations provide opportunities for personal growth, shared interests, and new experiences.

Support of Natural Systems

The support of natural systems in our life is fundamental to our well-being and survival. These systems are essential for our survival, prosperity, and quality of life. We need to be aware of the invaluable support from natural systems.

- **Air Quality:** The atmosphere sustains life by providing the air we breathe. Natural systems help maintain air quality by absorbing pollutants and producing oxygen through photosynthesis, ensuring a healthy environment for human health.
- **Water Resources:** Rivers, lakes, and groundwater systems are crucial sources of freshwater for drinking, agriculture, and industrial use. Natural systems play a vital role in water purification, ensuring the availability of clean water for human consumption.
- **Climate Regulation:** Natural systems, such as forests and oceans act to regulate the Earth's climate.
- **Food Production:** Ecosystems, such as agricultural lands provide us with essential food resources.
- **Biodiversity:** Natural systems support diverse flora and fauna, contributing to biodiversity.
- **Natural Disaster Mitigation:** Ecosystems, like wetlands and mangroves, act as natural buffers against floods, storms, and other natural disasters, protecting human settlements from potential harm.
- **Wellness:** Natural environments, such as green spaces, offer valuable opportunities and promote mental and physical well-being.
- **Soil Fertility:** Natural systems contribute to soil fertility through nutrient cycling and organic matter decomposition, essential for sustaining plant life.
- **Pollination:** Natural systems support pollinators like bees and butterflies, which are critical for crop production and the reproduction of many plant species.

Support of Manmade Systems

The support of manmade systems in our life has revolutionized the way we live, work, and interact with the world around us. These systems, created through human ingenuity and innovation, are integral to our lives and significantly support us.

The support of manmade systems has further elevated our capabilities, improved living standards, and created opportunities for growth and progress.

- **Transportation Systems:** Transportation networks, including roads, railways, airplanes, and ships, connect people and goods across vast distances, enabling efficient movement and trade.
- **Communication Systems:** Technologies like the internet and social media have revolutionized communication, allowing instant and global connectivity, information sharing, and collaboration.
- **Healthcare Systems:** Healthcare systems and medical research, provide essential medical services, advanced treatments, and life-saving interventions.
- **Educational Systems:** Schools, colleges, and universities foster learning, knowledge dissemination, and personal development, empowering individuals to pursue their goals.
- **Energy Systems:** Energy infrastructure, including power plants, electricity grids, and renewable energy sources, provide the energy needed to power homes, industries, and technology.
- **Economic Systems:** Economic structures, such as financial institutions, markets, and trade systems, facilitate economic activities, job opportunities, and wealth generation.
- **Governance Systems:** Including laws, institutions, and political structures, create order, protect rights, and ensure the functioning of societies.
- **Housing Systems:** Provide shelter and living spaces, promoting comfort, safety, and community development.

- **Industrial Systems:** Industrial processes and manufacturing systems produce goods and products that meet the diverse needs and demands of society.
- **Information Systems:** Systems for data transfer, data storage, analysis, and retrieval have transformed the way information is managed, leading to advancements in research, science, and decision-making.

Support of Non-living Things

Every day, the things surrounding us silently contribute to our well-being, making life comfortable and convenient. Though they may be labeled as non-living, their support is invaluable. By easing our daily tasks and adding joy to our existence, they enable us to focus on personal growth, relationships, and pursuing our passions. These precious gifts are often taken for granted, urging us to be mindful of the abundance that surrounds us.

- **Food:** Fruits, vegetables, grains, and other items provide us with essential nutrients and energy for our bodies to function.
- **House:** Structures like houses and apartments give us shelter and protection, providing a safe and comfortable living space.
- **Clothing:** Clothes and shoes keep us warm, protected, and comfortable in different weather conditions.
- **Home Gadgets:** Refrigerators, cooking utensils, washing machines, microwave ovens and other items make household tasks more convenient and efficient.
- **Electronic Gadgets:** Electronic devices like televisions, music systems and others provide entertainment, information, and communication.
- **Vehicles:** Cars, bikes, buses and other vehicles allow us to travel and commute over long distances quickly and comfortably.
- **Computing Devices:** Laptops and desktops aid in various tasks, such as work, education, and entertainment.

- **Personal Gadgets:** Cellphones, watches, fitness trackers, and other gadgets help us monitor and manage our health and daily activities.

Deep within us, we hold the knowledge of these precious blessings, yet amidst life's chaos, we tend to overlook their significance. Oh, how they deserve our attention! Let us never ignore their presence, for when we embrace them with gratitude, they bloom into even greater wonders, enriching every corner of our existence.

From the serene smile greeting a new day to the captivating sunset, we savor each moment with gratitude. In the day's journey, we appreciate supportive colleagues, nutritious meals, and moments of laughter. Our awareness extends to the support of family, the comfort of home, and the joy of pursuing passions. Amidst challenges, we cherish learning opportunities that foster growth.

CHAPTER 7

FIND OUR FOOTING: SELF ASSESSMENT

"In the depths of winter, I finally learned that within me there lay an invincible summer."

– Albert Camus

Understanding where we stand in our pursuit of happiness is vital, and that's where self-analysis and assessment come into play. Did you know that self-esteem and happiness go hand in hand? When we have a healthy self-esteem, it often leads to a higher level of happiness. When we appreciate more, we have good self-esteem.

To measure our happiness index, we can do some introspection and reflection. This helps us identify areas where we can improve and take proactive steps to increase our happiness. By regularly assessing our happiness index, we can make sure we're on track to lead a more fulfilling and satisfying life.

Self-esteem is all about how much we value and believe in ourselves. Having a confident view of ourselves is crucial, as it affects our relationships, mental health, and overall well-being. To measure it, we can use a self-esteem index (**SEI**). It's a tool with questions or statements for us to respond to using a rating scale. The final score from our responses shows our level of self-esteem. It will help us understand ourselves better and guide us towards a happier life.

A good SEI can only ensure overall happiness, which is a common goal for many individuals. To determine our SEI, we can evaluate ourselves in seven areas and score each area on a scale of 1 to 10, with 1 being the lowest and 10 being the highest. These areas include:

1. **Gratitude index:** The Gratitude Index refers to an individual's level of appreciation and thankfulness towards different aspects of their life. To assess the SEI related to gratitude, individuals can analyse their gratitude index using the five heads: *mind, body, people, systems, and things.* The mind head encompasses gratitude for mental abilities while the body head involves being grateful for physical health and capabilities. Gratitude towards people involves recognizing the contributions of individuals in one's life. The systems head refers to appreciating natural and societal systems that enhance quality of life, and the things head involves gratitude for material possessions and resources. By assessing gratitude in these areas, individuals can cultivate a mindset of appreciation and enhance their overall well-being.

   Let us score our SEI on the *five heads** of gratitude, and see how much we are grateful amidst challenges and difficulties.

2. **Self talk:** Self-talk refers to the internal dialogue that occurs within an individual's mind. It can greatly impact our SEI, and it is important to check the nature of our thoughts in order to assess our SEI related to self-talk.

   Only empowering self-talk will add a score to our SEI, as it can contribute to a healthier and more creative mindset. Disappointed self-talk, on the other hand, can diminish our sense of self-worth and adversely impact our SEI.

3. **Score in primary roles:** To ensure harmonious functioning in the primary roles of our life, it is crucial to lead an action-oriented lifestyle on a daily basis. Evaluating our performance in each role can help score our SEI within those specific domains. The four primary roles to consider are our role as a child, in occupation, as a spouse, and as a parent. We need to evaluate our performance in the roles that are applicable to us.

   It is important to note that only our actions to maintain harmony in these four primary roles will add a score to our SEI.

4. **Schedule in daily life:** Incorporating time for personal growth and self-care within our daily routine is essential for a fulfilling life. By evaluating our SEI in relation to our schedule's four key time slots—morning, office, evening, and bedtime—we can determine if we are effectively allocating time for self-improvement.

   We need to check our *four time slots** and score our SEI in each of these slots to determine how well we are utilising our time.

5. **Chain of Goodness(COG):** It refers to the uplifting impact that can be created through everyday acts of grace and unconditional giving. To assess our SEI related to COG, we need to evaluate our daily activities and determine how much we are contributing through GAUGE(Graceful and Unconditional Giving Everyday).

We need to start by evaluating our contributions in our *primary roles**, and then venture into finding ways to extend kindness to others as well.

6. **Ownership:** Ownership is taking responsibility for one's actions and circumstances, and taking action to improve them. It involves being accountable, decisive, and proactive.

   In the absence of ownership, "Cry baby/belly acher syndrome" emerges because the person feels helpless or powerless to change their circumstances. Without a sense of control or responsibility, they may feel that they have no agency in the situation and become overwhelmed by crippling emotions. Instead of taking action to improve the situation, they may complain or blame others for their difficulties, which can perpetuate a self-destructive cycle.

   "Cry baby/belly acher syndrome" refers to a pattern of behaviour characterised by frequent crying, whether through tears, words, or thoughts. While crying can be a natural form of emotional release, persistent and prolonged episodes may indicate low self-esteem and a lack of awareness about life. This may manifest in behaviours such as making excuses, putting blame on others, and excessive complaining. It can have an adverse impact on our SEI.

   To evaluate SEI, we must assess our accountability and ownership in our actions.

7. **Resilience:** Resilience is the ability to recover quickly from difficult situations. It involves being able to bounce back from adversity and continue moving forward, even when faced with challenges. It is not just about being tough or never experiencing harmful emotions. It is about being able to adapt to change and overcome obstacles, while also acknowledging and processing difficult emotions.

In contrast, vulnerability refers to the state of being exposed to emotional or physical harm. It is a natural human experience and can be measured by the frequency and duration of exposure to difficult situations in our day-to-day lives. However, vulnerability is not the opposite of resilience. In fact, developing resilience requires acknowledging and working through feelings of vulnerability and discomfort.

Our SEI is influenced by our ability to demonstrate resilience in the face of vulnerability.

Having strong resilience can significantly impact the Self-Esteem Index.

The results of assessing our SEI across the various dimensions discussed above can provide insight into our overall sense of self-worth and satisfaction with our life. A score of ***around eight*** in each of the above dimensions is considered good, as it indicates a level of consistency in action-oriented behaviour and a commitment to personal growth.

Achieving a consistently high SEI is an ongoing process that requires regular self-reflection and a commitment to taking actions that promote personal well-being.

Note: Engaging in day-to-day activities solely out of compliance, compulsion, or virtue signaling can adversely impact our self-esteem.

- ***Five heads of Gratitude***: Mind, Body, People, Systems and Things
- ***Four time slots:*** Morning time, Office time, Evening time and Bedtime
- ***Primary Roles***: Child, Occupational, Spouse and Parent

Self Esteem Measurement Parameters

Score sheet

Parameters		Score
Gratitude index	**Head-1**	
	Head-2	
	Head-3	
	Head-4	
	Head-5	
Self talk		
Score in primary roles	**Role-1**	
	Role-2	
	Role-3	
	Role-4	
Schedule in daily life	**Slot-1**	
	Slot-2	
	Slot-3	
	Slot-4	
Chain of Goodness(COG)		
Ownership		
Resilience		

CHAPTER 8

CONSTRAINTS

"The unexamined life is not worth living."

– Socrates

As we continue on our quest for creating awareness about happiness, we come across a significant challenge – constraints. They come in the form of conditioning, which is a powerful force that shapes us from the very beginning of our lives. It's a combination of nature, tradition and environment that influence who we become. But here's the catch – this conditioning can sometimes act as a formidable barrier on our path to true happiness.

From the time we are born, we start absorbing beliefs, attitudes, and behaviours from the world around us. This conditioning comes from our families, our practices, and the people we interact with. It becomes a part of us, and we may even cling to it, thinking it defines who we are. But here's the truth – real ownership of our lives comes from consciously designing and shaping it based on our own values and vision.

A closer look tells us that it comes in two main aspects: habits and thoughts. Some of it is easy to spot, like the habits we develop or the thoughts that occupy our minds. But there's also conditioning that's more subtle, influencing us in ways we might not even notice.

It's important to understand that not all conditioning is "bad." Some of it can be beneficial, empowering us and bringing joy to our lives. But there's also conditioning that limits us, holding us back from reaching our full potential.

To break free from these constraints, we need to become aware of the influence of conditioning on our lives, peeling back the layers to see what truly shapes us.

Consider some examples to help us better understand how analyzing our conditioning can uncover the factors that might be holding us back from achieving our fullest potential in life. This journey of self-discovery will empower us to break free from the constraints and create a life that aligns with our deepest desires and aspirations. The following matrix depicts some of the most common types of conditioning an individual has. The type of conditioning determines its subtlety - how obvious it is to the perception. The effect of conditioning determines its default impact in one's life.

Conditioning Matrix

Conditioning	Details	Type	Effect	Remarks
Food	Adhering to a specific dietary group based on the existing practices around.	Evident	Limiting	Overlooking the chance to discover a wide range of culinary options.
Clothing	Using clothing tailored to a specific region or locale.	Evident	Limiting	Neglecting the numerous clothing options that can provide enhanced comfort for oneself.
Creativity - Language	Acquired through the process of upbringing.	Evident	Expanding	It is important to have a willingness to learn additional languages when necessary.
Creativity-Music	Music is a universal form of conditioning that transcends boundaries worldwide.	Evident	Expanding	Music is an inherent instinct within human beings, and it is important to examine any potential obsessions associated with it.
Creativity-Singing	Singing is acquired during the process of upbringing for certain individuals.	Evident	Expanding	It is truly delightful to derive joy from singing while maintaining a harmonious balance with other activities.
Creativity-Dance	Dance is an inherent inclination found in the majority of individuals.	Subtle	Expanding	Engaging in uninhibited dancing brings about a sense of expansion in our lives.
Weak Emotional Intelligence (EI)	Numerous individuals exhibit limited emotional intelligence, influenced by their surrounding environment.	Subtle	Limiting	This stands as a significant obstacle on the journey towards sustainable happiness, as its subtle nature makes it challenging to discern.

Conditioning	Details	Type	Effect	Remarks
Morning routine	This habit is deeply ingrained, acquired during the upbringing process.	Subtle	Limiting	Its subtlety and limitations arise from the absence of formal teaching in most societies.
Mortality phobia	Instilled in one's thinking during the process of upbringing.	Evident	Limiting	Mortality is an inherent part of life, and allowing fear of it to dominate our mindset prevents us from the numerous possibilities in life.
Money	The significance of money as a valuable resource is ingrained worldwide through deep-rooted conditioning.	Evident	Limiting	Money serves as just one pathway to happiness, as there are numerous other blessings that are equally essential for a fulfilled life. Overemphasizing the importance of money tends to overshadow the significance of these other blessings required for true happiness.
Wellness	The definition of wellness is often confined to material resources.	Evident	Limiting	Comprehensive wellness, which includes physical health, mental well-being, and healthy relationships, is often overlooked by many individuals in terms of its importance.
Actions	The actions we engage in as part of our daily routines are often acquired in a random or disorganized manner.	Subtle	Limiting	Our actions can lead to significant losses when we perform them without recognizing the long-term limiting impact they may have on our lives.
Cleanliness	Maintaining cleanliness of both our bodies and our surroundings is a deeply ingrained practice.	Subtle	Limiting	Due to our familiarity with it, we often fail to recognize the restricting behaviours associated with this habit. Some remain unaware of its impact, while others develop an excessive attachment to it.

Conditioning	Details	Type	Effect	Remarks
Exoticism	It is commonly observed in developing nations, where there is a tendency to idolize economically prosperous countries and admire everything about them.	Subtle	Limiting	Restricting one's thinking to a singular idea based solely on a specific aspect of available resources obstructs the exploration of numerous abundant possibilities. This tendency often stems from a long history of poverty, which can result in a diminished mental state.
Virtue signaling	Maintaining face value is often referred to as virtue signaling, indicating that the individual involved is primarily focused on self-promotion and demonstrating their own righteousness, rather than genuinely addressing the underlying issues.	Subtle	Limiting	Considerable amounts of invaluable life energy, time, and resources are invested in virtue signaling, often resulting in missed opportunities and unexplored possibilities.
Lethargy	Lethargy can be further reinforced through societal influences and the availability of modern conveniences, contributing to its natural conditioning.	Subtle	Limiting	It is a tricky way of mind as the logic behind it is hard to refute. While seeking comfort is a fundamental human instinct, an unawareness of its unforeseen consequences can significantly constrain us, hindering our exploration of numerous possibilities in life and limiting our potential.

Conditioning	Details	Type	Effect	Remarks
Gender Identity	Individuals are typically influenced by environmental factors in the formation of their gender identity. The identification of most individuals is often based on their reproductive capacities.	Subtle	Limiting	The limitation of conditioning based on a singular aspect of individuals' sexuality prevents them from exploring the vast range of possibilities and potential inherent within each human being.

I want to share some instances relevant nowadays about conditioning that can impact our pursuit of happiness. These challenges might be familiar to us, so we'll take a closer look at them.

First, we have the overconsumption of information and entertainment. In today's digital world, we have so much information and fun stuff at our fingertips. But sometimes, it can get overwhelming, and we end up feeling distracted all the time.

Next to mention are hyper palatable foods. These are those super tasty, processed foods that we can't resist. They might be yummy, but they can lead to overeating and have damaging effects on our health in the long run.

Lastly, there are obsessions. These are like those persistent thoughts or desires that just won't leave us alone. Maybe it's being fixated on relationships, success at work, having lots of things, or even substances that can mess with our happiness and well-being.

The good news is that once we recognize these hurdles, we can work on overcoming them.

SECTION B:

THE BENEFIT BLUEPRINT: MAPPING THE PATH TO ABUNDANT REWARDS

CHAPTER 9

THE ODYSSEY BEGINS

"He who knows others is wise; he who knows himself is enlightened."

– Lao Tzu

Visualize Life's Symphony

When we think about the meaning of life, we often realize that sustainable happiness is what really matters at its core. That means our actions, decisions, and the things we pursue are all driven by the desire to be happy and fulfilled. By picturing our purpose, we understand that true contentment and joy come from living our lives in a way that makes us happy. This process of visualizing helps us see the right path to take, so we can work towards creating a life filled with experiences and values that lead to genuine happiness.

Let's take a closer look at the two important steps that lead to sustainable happiness:

Step 1: Acknowledging the abundance of blessings

We find ourselves in possession of a multitude of valuable gifts that contribute to our lives. Our mental and physical health stand as pillars of well-being, while the presence of cherished relationships and the support we receive enhance our daily experiences. The beauty and intricacies of nature further enrich our surroundings. Beyond this, we are granted opportunities to grow, freedoms that enable us to shape our paths, and material possessions that contribute to our comfort. It remains imperative to cultivate a sense of awareness regarding these blessings and their significance, thereby nurturing a deep understanding of the many elements that shape our existence.

Step 2: Identifying and Appreciating Smaller Events

While significant goals and accomplishments hold their place, enduring happiness emerges from discovering delight within the smaller, routine moments of life. Being aware and mindful enables us to recognize and treasure these occurrences. By actively embracing and valuing these modest sources of happiness that frequently cross our paths, we cultivate an empowering perspective and a deepened awareness of life's richness.

For example, spending quality time with near ones, doing things we love, enjoying nature, being kind to others, celebrating our daily accompaniments, or simply enjoying peaceful moments can all bring happiness. By paying attention to and cherishing these moments, we can create a sense of happiness and contentment in our daily lives.

Sustainable happiness is not something we achieve once and forget about; it's an ongoing journey. It requires us to reflect on ourselves, commit to personal growth, and make a conscious effort to prioritize our well-being. By visualizing our purpose and appreciating the small events that bring happiness, we lay a strong foundation for a fulfilling and joyous life. So, let's keep moving forward on this journey towards happiness and fulfillment.

Chapter 10

KEY TERRAIN

"Simplicity is the ultimate sophistication."

– ***Confucius***

The Essence Within

As we journey through life, we need to realise that we are at the center of it all. Our happiness and personal growth are very important. We need to take care of ourselves from the inside out. To do this, we need to understand our inner selves and work hard to overcome any challenges that come our way. These challenges might be things we think about ourselves, limiting thoughts, or outside problems that stop us from moving forward.

Getting to know our inner selves means looking deep into our thoughts, feelings, and what we believe in. We have to think about how we can improve and grow. This can free us from anything that's holding us back and foster a happier and more empowering inner self.

Overcoming hurdles and growing as a person is a journey that never really ends. We need to take action to face our fears, doubts, and insecurities, being strong and determined, resilient against challenges and working towards becoming the best version of ourselves. We can use helpful practices like personal development programs to make progress.

Getting stronger inside is significantly important because it helps us handle all the things life throws at us. When we focus on our growth and well-being, we become better at dealing with challenges and responsibilities. We might acquire new knowledge and uphold a hopeful mindset, leading to continuous personal growth. So, let's look inside, work on ourselves, and be the best we can be.

Role Blueprint

As we seek happiness in life, we frequently encounter challenges, particularly due to the diverse roles we hold. Whether as a child, a parent, a spouse, or in a professional capacity, each role brings a multitude of responsibilities and expectations. Yet, at times, we find ourselves lacking proper training or clear guidance on effectively managing these roles.

Because of this, we might feel stuck or overwhelmed while dealing with these responsibilities. And that can stop us from being truly happy and content. When we don't know how to manage our roles properly, it becomes tough to enjoy the little moments in life that bring us happiness.

If we keep living like this, with too much stress and dissatisfaction from our roles, life can feel boring and draining. So, it's essential to learn and grow, to become better at handling our roles. We need to learn how to manage our responsibilities, take care of ourselves, and set healthy boundaries.

Even though we juggle multiple roles simultaneously and interact with various individuals, it's crucial to recognize our shared essence across every role. Therefore, it becomes essential to wholeheartedly engage in each role, contributing to a harmonious atmosphere in every aspect of our lives

When we invest in learning how to handle our roles well, life becomes easier. We can reduce stress and make room for the little moments that make us happy. Also, doing things that bring us joy and being mindful can help us handle our roles better and have a more balanced and fulfilling life.

Chapter 11

HAPPINESS PATHFINDERS

"Our actions are determinants of our happiness."

PWP - Preparation of War in Peace

In our minds, we know it's crucial to prepare ourselves for what lies ahead. In this context, we can learn a big lesson from the defense forces. They get ready for war even when there is peace because they know being prepared is very important. Just like them, we need to be fully capable of dealing with any challenges that show up in our lives. Let's give it a special name - "Preparation of war in peace". It means being ready before anything tough happens, just like the defense forces do.

Imagine an athlete who wants to win a big race. To have the best chance of winning, they don't just show up on the day of the race without any practice. Instead, they train hard, eat well, and get enough rest. This is preparing for war in peace. By putting in the effort and getting ready ahead of time, they increase their chances of success when the important moment comes.

Similarly, think about a student who has an important exam coming up. Instead of waiting until the last minute to study, they start preparing early. They review their notes, do practice tests, and ask their teacher for help if needed. This way, they feel confident and ready when the exam day arrives. This is preparing for war in peace - getting ready before the big challenge comes.

In our daily lives, there are many situations where being prepared can make a huge difference. For example, if we have a presentation to give at work, practicing beforehand and knowing our material well can help us feel less nervous and do our best. Or, if our family plans a camping trip, packing everything we need in advance and learning camping skills will make the experience more enjoyable and stress-free.

Being prepared also applies to unexpected situations. Let's say there's a sudden power outage in your Neighbourhood. If we have a flashlight and some candles ready, we won't be left in the dark, feeling scared or worried.

So, "Preparation of war in peace" means taking the time to get ready for challenges before they happen. This helps us in facing uncertainties with confidence, overcoming obstacles more easily, and having a greater chance of success in our endeavors.

To do this, we use powerful visualisation techniques. It's like watching a movie in our minds, where we imagine ourselves overcoming challenges with confidence and strength. With this mental practice, we train our minds to respond quickly and effectively when we face difficulties.

We also need to focus on continuous learning and personal growth. Learning new things and developing skills are like our secret weapons for the future. By staying curious and open to new opportunities, we become more adaptable and ready to face whatever comes our way.

Emotional preparedness is another essential part of our plan. We believe that we can stay calm and strong even when things get tough. We know that we have the inner resources and abilities to handle challenges and bounce back from setbacks.

Here are some examples of how preparedness can be useful.

- **Financial Preparedness:** Financial preparedness involves making smart choices with our money, emphasizing sensible expenditure to ensure we can save and invest for the time ahead. It serves as a safety net for unexpected situations, reducing stress and ensuring stability during tough times like job loss or other exigency. Prioritizing sensible expenditure helps avoid unnecessary debt and builds a financial cushion. By being financially prepared, we gain control over our finances and have the confidence to handle challenges effectively. It doesn't eliminate difficulties, but it empowers us to navigate uncertainties with ease.
- **Health and Wellness Preparedness**: Taking care of our physical and mental health is very important. Eating healthy, ensuring enough body movement, and prioritizing self-care protect us from potential health issues.
- **Personal Development Preparedness**: Continuous learning and developing new skills make us adaptable and versatile, helping us navigate career changes or unexpected situations with ease.
- **Relationship Preparedness:** Building strong and healthy relationships requires streamlined effort and preparedness. Effective communication, active listening, and emotional intelligence are tools that help us handle relationship challenges in an effective way.
- **Goal Setting and Action Plan**: It is vital for achieving success. They provide a roadmap to turn aspirations into reality. Setting clear goals and outlining steps to reach them enhances motivation, direction, and

focus. This approach optimizes resources and tracks progress, leading to meaningful accomplishments and personal growth.

We need to acknowledge the power of preparedness and be ready for whatever life brings our way. With our preparedness, we can conquer challenges and emerge stronger.

Let's make things easier to understand and talk about the idea of "**Preparation of war in peace**" in our personal lives. We'll use three simple stories to help us see the importance of preparedness.

Maya was passionate about her career as a graphic designer. She loved her job and it brought a sense of fulfilment in her. However, Maya had heard instances of unexpected layoffs in her industry, which made her realise the importance of being prepared for any unforeseen challenges.

Keeping these in mind, Maya decided to take proactive measures. She began by building an emergency fund, diligently setting aside a portion of her income each month by learning and practicing sensible expenditure. This fund would serve as a financial cushion in case she faced sudden unemployment or a decrease in clients.

Maya also recognized the need to stay updated with the latest trends and technologies in graphic design. She enrolled in online courses, attended design conferences, and actively sought opportunities to enhance her skills. By continuously learning and expanding her expertise, she ensured that she remained competitive in the ever-evolving design industry.

In addition to her professional development, Maya focused on nurturing relationships within her industry. She regularly attended networking events, volunteered for design organisations, and connected with fellow designers. Building a strong professional network would not only provide support during challenging times but also open doors to potential job opportunities or freelance projects.

As Maya prepared herself, she also cultivated emotional strength and adopted an empowering mindset. Maya knew that challenges could arise unexpectedly, but she believed in her ability to adapt and find new opportunities amidst adversity. This strength would serve her well in navigating any unexpected twists in her career journey.

One day, Maya's worst fear came true when her company faced financial difficulties and had to downsize. Despite the shock and uncertainty, Maya was prepared. She relied on her emergency fund to cover her living expenses while she actively pursued new job opportunities. Her continuous learning and strong professional network paid off as she quickly connected with potential employers and secured freelance projects to sustain her income.

During this challenging period, Maya's emotional strength shone through. She remained focused and maintained a constructive outlook. With each setback, she saw an opportunity for growth and utilised her newfound time to further enhance her skills and explore new design avenues.

Eventually, Maya landed a new job at a design agency that aligned perfectly with her goals and values. Her preparedness had paid off, not only in helping her navigate the challenges of unexpected job loss but also in positioning her for a brighter and more fulfilling career path.

Maya's story serves as a powerful reminder that preparedness is a mindset and a proactive approach to life. By imbibing preparedness, we can navigate unexpected twists and turns with confidence and the ability to transform challenges into opportunities. It reminds us to prioritise financial stability, continuous learning, meaningful relationships, and emotional well-being, creating a strong foundation for a fulfilling and successful life journey.

Nob and Reni had been together for several years. Their relationship was built on a strong bond and a shared commitment to its long-term success. They understood that unforeseen challenges could arise at any point and recognized the importance of being prepared.

To proactively prepare for future issues, Nob and Reni made it a habit to engage in regular relationship check-ins and discussions. They set aside dedicated time to openly communicate about their expectations, needs, and aspirations. With an open mind, they addressed potential areas of conflict or concern, seeking to understand each other's perspectives and finding mutually agreeable solutions well in advance.

In their script of preparedness, they understood the value of continuous personal growth and learning. They understood that relying solely on external support may not always be feasible or available. They actively sought out resources such as relationship books, workshops, and self-reflection to develop skills in effective communication, conflict resolution, and emotional intelligence. They invested time and effort into understanding themselves and each other, building a strong foundation of self-awareness and empathy.

They had meticulously fortified their bond, having readied themselves for the challenges their relationship might face. One such formidable trial emerged when a longstanding misunderstanding between them erupted into a heated argument, threatening to fracture the foundation of their connection.

In the heat of the moment, harsh words were exchanged, and emotions ran high. It seemed as though their unity was hanging by a thread, poised to unravel. Yet, the groundwork they had laid for their relationship began to reveal its strength. Drawing from their preparedness, they both took a step back to cool their tempers and gain perspective.

In another instance, the strong foundation of trust and preparation that they had diligently cultivated faced an unexpected test. Nob caught sight of Reni in the company of another man, engrossed in joyful conversation and shared laughter. The scene sparked a seed of doubt in his mind, unsettling his thoughts and emotions.

Despite the initial shock and unease, he recognized the importance of addressing his feelings rather than allowing them to fester. He approached Reni in a composed and open manner.

Choosing a calm and private setting, he gently expressed his observations and the emotions they had stirred within him. Reni, appreciating his honesty, responded candidly, explaining that the man was a childhood friend she hadn't seen in years. She reassured him of their unwavering bond and clarified any misconceptions that had arisen.

Nob's decision to communicate rather than jump to conclusions allowed them to engage in a heartfelt dialogue. This open conversation not only assuaged his doubts but also deepened their mutual understanding. The incident served as a reminder of the importance of trust and the strength of their relationship's foundation.

Their preparedness in handling relationship issues allowed them to recover swiftly and maintain a strong bond. By actively nurturing their relationships and addressing challenges promptly, they grew both individually and as a couple. Their commitment to being ready fostered lasting connections.

Jai understood that life could sometimes be overwhelming, with unexpected twists and turns. He recognized that being emotionally prepared was just as important as being physically prepared. Jai acknowledged that his emotions were an integral part of his well-being.

He took the time to connect with himself, exploring his thoughts and feelings in moments of solitude. He practiced self-reflection, allowing himself to fully experience each emotion that arose within him. He learned to accept both joy and grief, recognizing that each emotion carried valuable lessons and insights.

He knew that life's difficulties could take a toll on his emotional well-being. So, he developed coping strategies to help him bounce back from setbacks. He turned to activities that brought him joy, such as playing music, painting, and spending time in nature. These pursuits served as outlets for his emotions and helped him find solace and inner strength.

Jai understood the importance of building a supportive environment for himself through his preparedness. Recognizing the significance of having a support system, he actively sought out meaningful connections with friends and family. In their presence, he found a safe space to openly express his emotions, knowing that he would be met with understanding and acceptance.

They became his pillars of strength during both difficult and joyous times, offering a listening ear, valuable advice, and support. His commitment to cultivating a strong support system allowed him to navigate life's ups and downs with a sense of belonging and reassurance, knowing that he was not alone in his journey.

Jai's strong dedication to emotional preparedness faced its most critical test when a routine medical examination revealed an unexpected lump. He realized the concern of the medical team regarding this lump. The potential gravity of a serious health issue cast a shadow of uncertainty over him, evoking emotions ranging from fear to worry. Yet, what distinguished Jai was his prior commitment to tending to his emotional well-being. Through proactive efforts, he had built a support network, developed coping strategies, and fostered a healthy mindset. This foundation equipped him to confront the situation with a level-headed approach, leveraging his emotional toolkit and seeking guidance from his loved ones.

Driven by unwavering determination, Jai proactively sought medical assistance and underwent necessary treatment. In navigating this journey, his cultivated emotional foundation enabled him to process, confront, and transcend the complexities of his healing process, exemplifying the profound influence of emotional readiness in surmounting adversity.

Throughout his medical journey, Jai's emotional preparedness shone brightly. He channeled his energies into understanding the situation, seeking expert advice, and making informed choices. Self-reflection and self-awareness were key components of his approach, enabling him to confront his fears constructively. While the outcome remained uncertain, his emotional stability offered him a solid footing to navigate the challenges that lay ahead.

Jai's experience underscores the significance of emotional readiness in facing life's unexpected trials, showcasing how an investment in emotional well-being can empower individuals to confront adversity with strength and grace.

Appreciation Ritual

Imagine a special treasure box filled with happiness, joy, and contentment. Guess what? We already have this right within us. It's called **gratitude**, and it has the power to transform our lives.

An appreciation ritual or gratitude practice is a transformative practice that cultivates gratefulness in our daily lives. By mindfully acknowledging and valuing the blessings, we create a space to savor the present moment and find contentment. This sacred ritual empowers us to shift our perspective towards optimism, fostering a ripple effect of joy and compassion in our own lives and the lives of others. Through heartfelt appreciation, we can unlock the power of gratitude.

Let me share a secret - practicing gratitude is like having a wonderful gift that can make our days brighter and lighter. It's not always easy to remember all the good things that happen in our busy lives, but when we take a moment to say "thank you" for the wonderful moments and blessings, something amazing happens.

Our minds are like detectives searching for clues about what's wrong or dangerous. It's a protective mechanism that helps keep us safe. But sometimes, it focuses too much on the perceived threats, making us feel sad or worried. That's when practicing gratitude comes to the rescue.

When we practice gratitude, it flips a switch in our minds. Suddenly, we start noticing all the little joys and kind acts around us, wearing special glasses that help us see the beauty and goodness in the world.

Imagine this - as we wake up in the morning, we relish the gentle warmth of the sun on our faces. With a smile, we reflect on three things we're truly grateful for - our loving family, our passion for music, or the joy of spending time exploring nature.

As we journey through our day, the reasons for gratitude keep multiplying. We appreciate the friendly bus driver's wave, savor the delectable lunch that brings delight to our tummies, and cherish the laughter shared with our near ones.

Gratitude even helps us feel better when things get tough. When we face difficult times, remembering the good things in life gives us strength and courage. It's a powerful shield that protects our inner being from sadness and keeps hope alive.

Benefit of Gratitude Practice

- **Increases happiness**: Regular gratitude practices have been shown to increase levels of happiness and overall life satisfaction. When people focus on what they are grateful for, they are more likely to have joyful experiences.
- **Reduces stress and anxiety**: Gratitude helps to reduce feelings of stress and anxiety, as it encourages people to focus towards more creativity. This shift in perspective can lead to a greater sense of calm and well-being.
- **Improves resilience**: Gratitude helps people to develop a greater sense of resilience, leading them to focus on the good things in their lives, even in the face of challenges. This can help people to bounce back more quickly from setbacks, and to approach life with a greater sense of optimism and hope.
- **Improves physical health**: Gratitude extends its positive influence beyond mental and emotional realms, encompassing a notable impact on physical well-being as well.
- **Enhances relationships**: Expressing gratitude to others can strengthen bonds and improve communication, leading to more fulfilling relationships. Gratitude can also help people to appreciate and value the people in their lives, leading to deeper connections and more meaningful relationships.

Anecdotes On Gratitude

The Boy Who Wanted More: *This is about a young boy who is never satisfied with what he has, and always wants more. One day, he meets an old man who teaches him about gratitude and how to be thankful for what he already has. The boy learns that by focusing on what he is grateful for, he can be happier and more content with his life.*

The Apple Tree: *There was a farmer who had an apple tree that stopped bearing fruit. The farmer is upset and wants to cut down the tree, but a wise old man tells him to be patient and grateful for the shade and beauty that the tree provides. The next year, the tree starts bearing fruit again, and the farmer realises the importance of being grateful for what he has, even if it is not what he wants.*

The Little Match Girl*: The focus lies a poor girl who is selling matches on the street on a cold winter night. She is cold, hungry, and afraid, but finds comfort in lighting her matches and dreaming about a warm, happy life. The story ends with the girl's resilience shining through, as she perseveres through her hardships and continues to inspire others to be thankful for what they have.*

The Generous Tree: *The story revolves around a tree that gives everything it has to a boy, from its branches for the boy to climb and play on, to its trunk for the boy to build a boat, to its very roots to make a house. The boy grows up and becomes an old man, and returns to the tree, which is now just a stump. The old man realises how grateful he is for everything the tree has given him, and is content to simply sit and rest on the stump.*

The Man in the Mirror: *The narrative delves into the life of a man who spends his life comparing himself to others and feeling envious of their successes and blessings. One day, he looks in the mirror and sees that he has been given many gifts and talents of his own, and realises how grateful he should be for what he has. The story encourages people to focus on their own blessings and to be thankful for what they have, rather than comparing themselves to others.*

The Wonder of Saying Thank You: *The focus shifts to a woman who learns the power of gratitude by saying "thank you" to everything in her life, from the sun that shines to the water that quenches her thirst. The woman realises that by expressing gratitude, she can attract more great things into her life, and that she can be happier and more content by focusing on what she is grateful for.*

The Grateful Dead: *Central to the narrative is a man who has been given a second chance at life after a near-death experience. The man decides to live his life with gratitude, and he finds that by focusing on what he is grateful for, he can be happier, more content, and more fulfilled.*

When we read such anecdotes about gratitude, something truly wonderful happens inside us. Our core blooms with gratefulness, and amazing things start to unfold in our lives, planting seeds of thankfulness. We start to see the world in a whole new way.

We can explore and read more anecdotes about thankfulness and allow goodness to flourish within us. With gratitude as our guide, we'll discover a world full of wonders and blessings, just waiting to be noticed and appreciated.

Here are some delightful examples of gratitude practices that have illuminated our world:

- **Ancient civilizations**: Many ancient civilizations, such as the Greeks and Romans, held festivals and ceremonies to give thanks for their blessings. These events were often accompanied by feasts, music, and offerings of food and other gifts.
- **American Thanksgiving**: The American holiday of Thanksgiving is a celebration of gratitude for the blessings of the harvest and of the year. The holiday originated with a feast held by the Pilgrims to give thanks for their safe arrival in the New World and for the bounty of the land.
- **The Japanese concept of Arigato**: The Japanese word Arigato is often used to express gratitude and thanks. This concept is deeply ingrained in Japanese culture, and is seen as a crucial part of building and maintaining relationships.

- **The African tradition of Ubuntu**: The African concept of Ubuntu is a belief in the interconnectedness of all people, and a recognition of the importance of gratitude and kindness in human relationships. Ubuntu emphasises the importance of looking out for each other and supporting one another, and is seen as a key factor in building strong, supportive communities.
- **The Chinese custom of gifting**: In Chinese culture, gift-giving is seen as a way to express gratitude and build relationships. Gifts are given on special occasions, such as holidays and birthdays, and are often accompanied by well-wishes and expressions of appreciation.
- **Gratitude in Native American culture**: Many Native American cultures have a strong tradition of gratitude and respect for the natural world. Through rituals and ceremonies, Native Americans have expressed their gratitude for the blessings of the land, the animals, and the elements, and have sought to maintain a harmonious relationship with the environment.
- **Hawaiian Ho'oponopono**: In Hawaiian culture, the practice of Ho'oponopono involves reconciliation and forgiveness. It is a way of expressing gratitude for the interconnectedness of all beings, seeking harmony, and offering forgiveness to maintain balance in relationships and communities.
- **Nigerian Kola Nut Offering**: In Nigerian cultures, the kola nut is considered a symbol of hospitality and gratitude. Offering kola nuts to guests or during special occasions is a way of expressing appreciation and welcoming others into the community.
- **South American Despacho Ceremony**: In various South American indigenous traditions, the despacho ceremony is performed as an offering and expression of gratitude to Pachamama (Mother Earth). Participants create intricate mandala-like offerings with various symbolic items, expressing thanks and harmony with nature.

- **The Indian tradition of Puja**: The tradition of puja in Indian culture is a revered practice that involves worship and acts of devotion. It is a way of expressing gratitude and reverence. Puja ceremonies, characterised by various practices and prayers, create a sacred space where individuals seek blessings, inner peace, and a deep connection. This cherished practice is an integral part of Indian tradition.
- **The tradition of "Hakarat Hatov"**: It is practiced in certain communities, emphasises recognizing the good in others and expressing gratitude for it. Originating from a particular cultural context, this concept, often expressed in the Hebrew language, underscores the significance of fostering strong relationships and maintaining an optimistic outlook on life.
- **The tradition of "shukr"**: Shukr is a cultural practice that emphasises expressing gratitude and thankfulness. It involves acknowledging the goodness and kindness received from others, fostering congenial relationships and contentment. Shukr includes verbal expressions of gratitude, acts of kindness, and recognizing the interconnectedness within communities. It encourages a mindful and appreciative outlook, recognizing life's blessings and joys, cultivating humility, compassion, and shared responsibility. Shukr reminds us to practice gratitude and appreciate the abundance of gifts and support that enhance our lives.
- **The Scandinavian custom of "takk"**: In Scandinavian cultures, gratitude is often expressed through the word "takk," which means "thank you." This simple word is used frequently in daily life as a way of expressing appreciation and gratitude for the help and support of others.
- **The Latin American tradition of "gracias"**: In Latin America, gratitude is often expressed through the word "gracias," which means "thank you." This simple word is used frequently in daily life as a way of acknowledging the kindness and generosity of others, and of expressing appreciation for the blessings of life.

- **The practice of "danksagung"**: In German-speaking cultures, gratitude is often expressed through the word "danksagung," which means "thanksgiving." This word is used in a variety of different contexts, from expressing appreciation for a gift or a kind act, to giving thanks for the blessings of life.
- **The Greek tradition of "eucharisteo"**: In ancient Greece, gratitude was expressed through the word "eucharisteo," which means "to give thanks." This word was used to describe a range of different experiences, from giving thanks for a bountiful harvest to expressing appreciation for the kindness of others.
- **Todah**: It is a concept found in ancient Near Eastern cultures, particularly in the region that encompasses modern-day Israel and its neighbouring areas. It represents a form of thanksgiving or gratitude in these cultural contexts. Todah is often associated with expressions of appreciation, acknowledgment, and offering thanks for blessings, acts of kindness, or deliverance from challenging circumstances.
- **The Native American tradition of "mitakuye oyasin"**: In many Native American cultures, gratitude is expressed through the phrase "mitakuye oyasin," which means "all are related." This phrase expresses the idea that everything in the world is interconnected, and that gratitude should be expressed for all of the relationships and connections that exist in life.
- **Itadakimasu**: This is a Japanese phrase commonly used before meals to express gratitude for the food being received. It reflects an acknowledgment of the efforts of those involved in producing the meal and the interconnectedness of all beings.
- **The Indian tradition of "dhanyavad"**: In India, gratitude is often expressed through the word "dhanyavad," which means "thank you." This simple word is used frequently in daily life as a way of acknowledging the kindness and generosity of others, and of expressing appreciation for the blessings of life.

- **The African tradition of "asante sana"**: In many African cultures, gratitude is expressed through the phrase "asante sana," which means "thank you very much." This phrase is used to express appreciation and gratitude for a wide range of experiences, from receiving a gift or help, to acknowledging the kindness of others.
- **The Australian tradition of "thanks a million"**: In Australia, gratitude is often expressed through the phrase "thanks a million," which is used to express a high level of appreciation and gratitude. This phrase is used in a variety of different contexts, from expressing gratitude for a gift or help, to acknowledging the kindness of others.
- **The British tradition of "ta very much"**: In Britain, gratitude is often expressed through the phrase "ta very much," which is a casual way of saying "thank you very much." This phrase is used frequently in daily life as a way of acknowledging the help and support of others, and of expressing appreciation for the blessings of life.
- **The French tradition of "merci beaucoup"**: In France, gratitude is often expressed through the phrase "merci beaucoup," which means "thank you very much." This phrase is used frequently in daily life as a way of acknowledging the kindness and generosity of others, and of expressing appreciation for the blessings of life.
- **The Italian tradition of "grazie mille"**: In Italy, gratitude is often expressed through the phrase "grazie mille," which means "thank you very much." This phrase is used frequently in daily life as a way of acknowledging the help and support of others, and of expressing appreciation for the blessings of life.
- **Gratitude letters**: The tradition of writing letters to express gratitude dates back to ancient times, when letters were often used to thank friends and family members for their kindness and support. Today, many people still write gratitude letters to express their appreciation for the things they're grateful for, whether it's to a family member, a friend, or even a complete stranger who has made a great impact on

their lives. These letters can have a profound impact on the recipient, and can help to build stronger relationships and foster feelings of goodwill and kindness.

- **Gratitude journals**: Throughout history, people have kept journals to reflect on their blessings and to express gratitude. These journals can be a powerful tool for cultivating an outlook for increasing feelings of happiness and well-being.

Are you ready to experience the wonderful benefits of meaningful rituals in your daily life? Let me introduce you to three incredible appreciation rituals that can easily become a part of your routine:

Gratitude Star

Envisage a special star that holds the power of gratitude within its shining points. I call it the "Gratitude Star," and it's a wonderful way to nurture gratitude in our lives.

Picture a five-pointed star in your mind, and each point represents something you are grateful for. It could be the loving support of your family and friends, the roof over your head, the tasty meals you enjoy, or even the beauty of nature that surrounds you.

By visualizing this Gratitude Star regularly, we remind ourselves to appreciate all the good things in our lives.

The best part is that the Gratitude Star is really easy to use. You can simply take a moment each day to think about what you are grateful for and assign it to one of the star's points. As you repeat this practice, you'll notice how it fills you with joy.

I've shared the Gratitude Star with many of my friends and loved ones, and they have all experienced its wonderful effects.

So, why not give the Gratitude Star a try? See its effect and watch how it transforms your perspective on life.

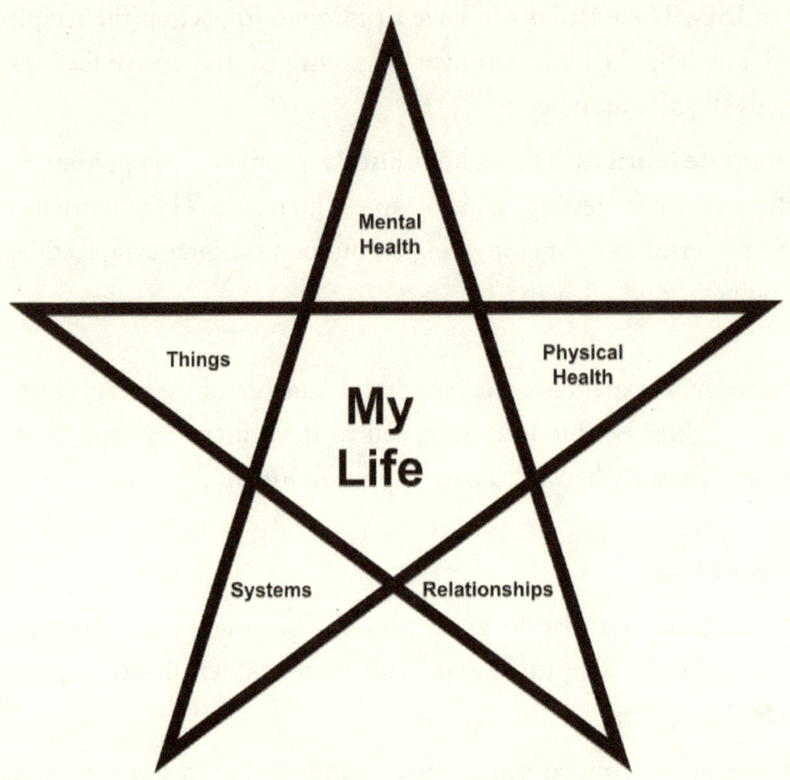

Imagine gazing into a wondrous star, shimmering brightly with the treasures of gratitude for every beautiful aspect of our life. This celestial marvel holds the key to cultivating profound thankfulness for the abundance that surrounds us.

As we fix our gaze upon the **first spike** of the star, we find ourselves immersed in the treasure of our mental health. Take a moment to admire this precious gift of a clear and vibrant mind, filled with boundless possibilities and emotions that colour our perception of the world. Let us be grateful for our ability to think, to feel, and to connect with others, for it is through our thoughts and emotions that we find meaning and purpose in our journey.

Shifting our attention to the **second spike**, we are met with a breathtaking revelation of the blessings of our physical health. In this moment of awareness and appreciation, we acknowledge the marvel of our bodies—the incredible gift of functioning sensory organs that allow us to see the vibrant colours of nature, to taste the sweetness of life's joys, and to feel the warmth of the touch of our near ones. We recognize the intricate systems within us that tirelessly work to sustain our well-being, enabling us to explore and revel in the wonders of existence.

Now, let us center our attention on the **third spike**, where we encounter the treasure of the people who have touched and shaped our lives. Here, we find a tapestry woven with the threads of care, support, and influence from those we hold dear. The care and guidance of our parents, the comforting presence of siblings, the uplifting friendships that brighten our days—all contribute to the colourful mosaic of our journey. But let us not forget the benevolent gestures of strangers, whose simple acts of kindness and influence have left lasting impressions on our lives. They may remain unknown to us, yet their valuable impact weaves itself into the fabric of our existence.

Raj never realized the significance of strangers in his life. He was a retired Air Force officer, known for his bravery and courage during his service days. One sunny day, as Raj was sitting on a bench in a park, looking deep in thought, a stranger approached him and waved.

Intrigued by the stranger's familiarity, Raj asked if they had met before. With a gentle smile, the stranger replied, 'We have never met, but I know you, Raj'.

Taken aback, Raj was puzzled. How could this stranger know him? Sensing Raj's confusion, the stranger began to narrate a remarkable incident that took place many years ago.

The stranger recounted a day when Raj was an Air Force officer, soaring high in the sky in his fighter plane. Life had a different plan that day, and Raj found himself in a life-threatening situation. He had to make a quick decision that would determine the outcome.

The stranger continued, explaining that they were a witness to that critical moment from afar. They had seen Raj's aircraft falter and had acted swiftly to summon rescue teams and provide crucial information about Raj's whereabouts.

Raj stood there, listening in awe as the stranger recounted the heroic efforts that had saved his life. It was like hearing a tale from a different realm, a realm where strangers turned out to be saviors in disguise.

Overwhelmed with gratitude, Raj thanked the stranger immensely. He realized that this encounter was more than just a chance meeting; it was a profound revelation about the nameless hero who had silently contributed to his well-being.

From that day forward, Raj carried with him a deep sense of appreciation for not just the known faces in his life, but also for the nameless heroes who had selflessly contributed to his safety.

The encounter with the stranger left Raj with a newfound appreciation for the countless blessings he had received, thanks to the kindness and preparedness of strangers who had touched his life in ways he could never have imagined.

The story of Raj and the stranger serves as a reminder that in the canvas of life, there are unsung heroes - people we may never meet again, but whose acts of compassion and preparedness leave an everlasting impact on our lives. Let us carry the spirit of gratitude and be thankful not only for the known faces but also for these nameless heroes who have woven threads of kindness into the fabric of our lives.

Continuing our practice of gratitude, let's now focus on the **fourth spike** of the star. It represents the incredible blessings we receive from the natural and man-made systems that support our lives. Take a moment to think about the earth's ecosystems that provide us with food and resources, and the intricate networks of infrastructure that make our daily lives easier. Let's express gratitude for the seamless functioning of these amazing systems that work tirelessly to ensure our well-being.

Moving on to the **fifth spike**, this represents the tangible aspects of our lives. Think about the food we eat that nourishes our bodies, the shelter that gives us comfort and safety, the vehicles that help us travel and explore, and the gadgets that enhance our productivity and keep us connected. Each of these material possessions is a blessing that makes our lives better in many ways.

By practicing gratitude for each spike of the star, we deepen our awareness of the countless blessings that surround us. From our mental and physical health to the people in our lives, the systems that sustain us, and the material aspects of our daily living, there's so much to be grateful for. This practice helps us see how interconnected and dependent we are on the world around us, fostering a profound sense of appreciation and gratitude.

As we continue with the Gratitude Star practice, we not only cultivate kindness but also nurture a spirit of unconditional giving. It transforms the star into a symbol of graceful and selfless generosity. This triggers GAUGE (**G**raceful **A**nd **U**nconditional **G**iving **E**veryday) and through its practice, we spread the profound effects of kindness and giving, creating a lasting impact on ourselves and those around us.

To make the most of this practice, consider printing out the gratitude star and placing it in a prominent spot in our homes, like the entrance or a common area. This will serve as a constant reminder to appreciate the abundance of blessings in our lives and amplify the impact of the practice.

An alternative approach is to adopt a similar practice using our hand, following the guidelines presented in the following figure.

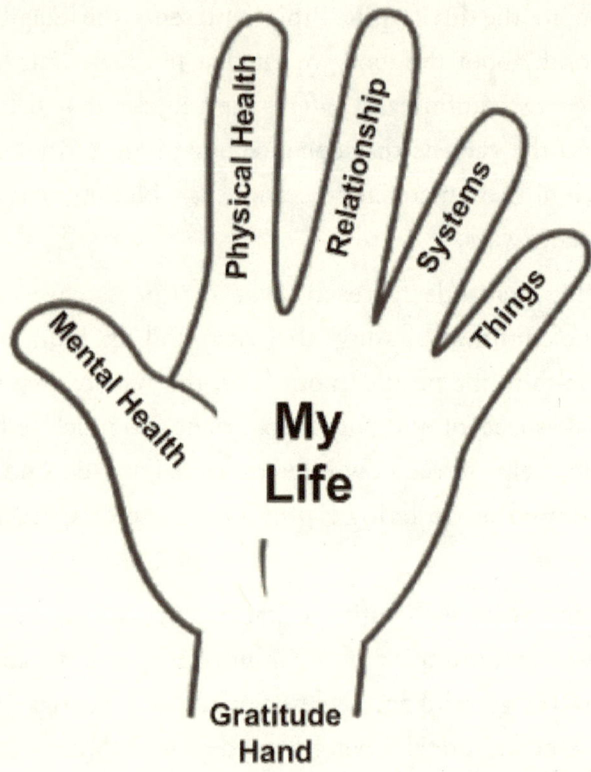

In the gratitude hand, each finger of the hand symbolizes a unique and precious aspect of the blessings in our lives. The thumb represents our mental health and well-being, acknowledging the importance of its capacity. The index finger signifies our physical health and vitality, recognizing the gift of a healthy body. The middle finger points to the people around us, such as family and friends, who enrich our lives with care and support. The ring finger represents the intricate natural and man-made systems that sustain us, from the Earth's ecosystems to the infrastructure that facilitates our daily lives. Lastly, the small finger signifies the materialistic things that bring us comfort and joy. Together, these fingers remind us of the abundance of blessings we have and inspire us to cultivate a deep sense of gratitude for each facet of our lives.

We can enhance this gratitude practice by incorporating the concept of "Low hanging fruit," as outlined in section A.

Gratitude Journal

This little book holds immense power to transform our lives and bring more joy and appreciation into our days. Life can get so busy and overwhelming at times. We might find ourselves focusing on what we don't have or the challenges we face, forgetting to notice the little joys and blessings all around us. That's where the power of a gratitude journal comes in. It gently nudges us to pause and take a moment each day to be mindful and appreciate the good things we already have.

It's incredible how this simple act of writing down our blessings can create big changes in our minds. It lifts our spirits and makes us feel happy. By training ourselves to seek out the beauty and goodness, even during tough times, we become masters in growing from our experiences.

It helps us grow and feel strong and we can handle anything that comes our way. The best part is that it makes us more aware of all the wonderful moments in our day. Those little things we might have missed before suddenly become so precious when we jot them down in our journal.

The key to start writing a gratitude journal is to make it a regular habit that suits our lifestyle. We can choose a pretty notebook or even an app on our phone.

Here are some ideas to get started:

- **Set aside dedicated time**: Designate a specific time each day or week to write in the gratitude journal. Consistency is key to reaping the benefits of this practice.
- **Start small**: Begin by writing down three to five things we are grateful for each day. They can be as simple as a sunny day, a supportive person, or a delicious meal. Gradually, we can expand the list or delve deeper into our reflections.
- **Be specific and detailed**: Instead of generic statements, provide specific details about why we are grateful for each item. This helps to deepen our appreciation and brings the experience to life on paper.

- **Reflect on the day or week**: Consider the joyful experiences, interactions, or moments that stood out for us. Reflect on how they made us feel and the impact they had on our well-being.
- **Embrace challenges and growth**: Let's not shy away from including moments of difficulty or adversity by including the lessons or insights we gained from those experiences and how they contributed to our personal growth.
- **Write freely and authentically**: Let our gratitude journal be a safe space for honest reflection. Allow our emotions, thoughts, and gratitude to flow naturally without judgement or pressure.

The main goal of writing a gratitude journal isn't to make it perfect or fancy, but to feel truly grateful. We don't need to worry about getting everything just right. The essence is to treat the journey as important and be grateful for the little things. As we keep writing in our journal, we'll start to see some amazing changes in how we look at life. We'll feel happier, more thankful, and our whole outlook will become brighter.

Gratitude Affirmation Prayer

I'm thrilled to introduce a fantastic practice that will fill us with joy and gratitude - the gratitude affirmation prayer. This amazing tool combines visualisation and affirmation to help us experience the abundance of blessings in our lives.

The first step is a simple mental shift. Instead of dwelling on what's lacking or worrying about what we don't have, we deliberately focus on the blessings we already possess. Once we've set our mindset on gratitude, we take the next step. We close our eyes and use the power of imagination to vividly visualize our blessings. Think of creating a movie in our minds, starring all the wonderful things that make us happy. From the people we love to the experiences we cherish, we relish every moment in this mental reel of gratitude.

We bring our emotions into play. As we visualize our blessings, we immerse ourselves in the feelings of joy, contentment, and appreciation reliving those happy moments all over again, making us swell with gratitude. We consciously and deliberately affirm the presence of these blessings in our lives saying, "Yes, I am blessed, and I am grateful". This powerful act of affirmation reinforces our conviction in the abundance that surrounds us, planting seeds of gratitude that grow into a beautiful garden of happiness.

As we make the Gratitude Affirmation Prayer a regular part of our lives, we create a ripple effect. Our days become infused with appreciation, and even the simplest moments become moments of celebration. We feel more connected to our near ones, and our relationships blossom with warmth and love.

We can practice the Gratitude Affirmation Prayer anytime, anywhere. Whether stuck in traffic or taking a break at work, a quick moment of gratitude can transform the mood and uplift the spirit.

We don't need complicated words or fancy techniques. Just focus on the everyday blessings that bring joy - the cozy bed we wake up in, the delicious food on our plate, or the sound of laughter shared with kin.

With the Gratitude Affirmation Prayer, we unlock the secret to true happiness. It's not about waiting for big moments; it's about finding joy in the little things. It's about living a life of abundance and appreciation, and it all starts with a simple prayer of gratitude.

Here are a few gratitude prayer examples that I recommend. We can create our own as well. It's important to remember that the purpose of this prayer is to cultivate happiness.

- I breathe in the gift of air, filling me with life and energy.
- I am thankful for the food I eat, nourishing and satisfying me.
- The sounds I hear bring joy and connection to my life.
- My legs carry me through life's journey, helping me explore and move forward.
- Through my eyes, I see the beauty that surrounds me.

- I appreciate the scents that come my way, awakening my senses.
- I feel the sensations on my skin, connecting me to the world.
- With gratitude, I use my voice to express my thoughts and connect with others.
- I appreciate the thoughts that come to my mind, allowing me to ponder and seek wisdom.
- Tasks and responsibilities come my way, and I embrace them willingly.
- Within the walls of my home, I find comfort and safety.
- I am grateful for the clothes I wear, providing comfort and modesty.
- I am grateful for the water that quenches my thirst.
- Education opens doors for me to learn and grow.
- Supportive people surround me, offering comfort and companionship.
- Laughter fills me with joy in life's simple moments.
- Affection reaches into my life, enabling me to both offer and accept.
- Creativity flows through me, igniting my passions.
- Good health blesses me with vitality and well-being.
- I cherish each moment, recognizing its value.
- Empathy guides my actions, showing kindness to others.
- Knowledge expands my understanding and broadens my horizons.
- Nature's beauty brings me peace and serenity.
- Diverse cultures enrich my life, teaching me new perspectives.
- Forgiveness sets me free from burdens of the past.
- Through self-expression, I share my voice and connect with others.
- Resilience helps me overcome challenges and grow stronger.
- Melodies uplift my spirit and bring joy.
- Exploring the world expands my horizons.
- I hold the power to make choices that shape my path.

- At night, I rest upon a bed, finding peaceful sleep and rejuvenation.
- Within this precious life, I find purpose and meaning.

With heartfelt gratitude, I appreciate the abundance in my life and recognize the blessings that surround me on my journey.

Intellectual Humility

It is said that "knowledge becomes a hurdle in knowing". Nowadays, people accumulate vast amounts of knowledge without grasping its relevance, preventing them from attaining the essential knowledge that could enrich their lives. In this process, they distance themselves from intellectual humility, which is crucial for leading a fulfilling life.

Intellectual humility is a valuable trait that can greatly benefit our personal lives. It involves recognizing our own limitations, being open to new ideas and perspectives, and developing a mindset of continuous learning and growth.

One of the significant benefits of intellectual humility is improved decision-making. When we are humble enough to acknowledge our biases and admit what we don't know, we become more receptive to feedback and different viewpoints. This openness allows us to make more informed decisions, avoid unnecessary mistakes, and build stronger connections with others.

Intellectual humility also nurtures a growth mindset, where we believe that with dedication and hard work, we can develop our abilities. When we recognize our own limitations, we are more likely to take on challenges and view failures as opportunities to learn and grow. This mindset empowers us to persevere through tough times and strive for continuous improvement.

It's common for people to expect intellectual humility from others while neglecting it in themselves. This double standard can hinder personal growth and effective communication. When we are quick to criticize others without acknowledging our own limitations, we risk becoming closed-minded and resistant to new ideas. This closed-off attitude can hinder our capacity to learn and develop, ultimately affecting our success and well-being.

To avoid inner conflict and promote personal growth, it's vital to align our beliefs and actions. Honesty with ourselves about our limitations and biases is crucial, and we must be willing to learn from others and admit when we are wrong. By maintaining consistency in our expectations of ourselves and others, we create a more authentic and open-minded approach to life.

When we imbibe intellectual humility, it also helps in building stronger relationships with others. Being open to learning from others and acknowledging our own mistakes makes us more approachable and trustworthy. This fosters deeper connections and more meaningful relationships with the people around us.

To develop intellectual humility, we can actively seek out new information, reassess our beliefs, and welcome feedback from others. Resolving any inner conflict that arises and using it as a catalyst for growth and learning will make us more self-aware, open-minded, and effective in both our personal and professional lives.

So how can individuals develop intellectual humility in their personal lives? Here are some tips:

- **Embrace the unknown**: Identify the required unknown area and be open to new ideas and perspectives, and recognize that there is always more to learn.
- **Listen actively**: Take the time to actively listen to others and seek to understand their point of view.
- **Seek feedback**: Ask others for feedback and be willing to accept constructive criticism.
- **Embrace uncertainty**: Recognize that there may be more than one right answer and that uncertainty is a natural part of the learning process.

- **Acknowledge mistakes**: Be willing to admit when we are wrong and take responsibility for our actions.

Intellectual Greed

When it comes to our approach to knowledge and learning, there are two distinct mindsets: intellectual humility and intellectual greed. These attitudes shape how we perceive and acquire information.

Intellectual humility is all about recognizing our own limitations and being open to learning from others, having a humble and open-minded outlook and valuing the quality of knowledge over the quantity. On the other hand, intellectual greed is driven by the desire for more and more knowledge, often without considering its reliability or usefulness. This approach may lead to a closed-minded attitude, where we value the sheer volume of information over its accuracy.

In today's digital age, where information is readily available, it's crucial to navigate through the overwhelming amount of data and focus on effective learning with intellectual humility. Here are some tips to do just that:

- **Seek Relevant and Credible Information**: Prioritize information that is relevant to your goals and backed by credible sources. This helps you make informed decisions and take effective action in your personal and professional life.
- **Be Critical: Don't take everything at face value**. Be critical of the information you come across. Ask questions, consider the source, and look for evidence that supports the claims being made.
- **Avoid Echo Chambers**: Don't just surround yourself with information that confirms your existing beliefs. Seek out diverse perspectives and engage with people who have different viewpoints. This helps broaden your understanding and encourages growth.
- **Practice Active Learning**: Engage actively with the information you're learning. Take notes, summarize key points, and ask questions. Actively

participating in the learning process helps you retain information and apply it effectively.

- **Embrace Humility**: Recognize that there's always more to learn, and it's okay not to have all the answers. Be willing to admit when you're wrong and seek feedback from others.

Developing intellectual humility is a journey that requires ongoing effort and self-reflection. By focusing on our own growth, showing understanding to others, and building meaningful relationships, we can create an inclusive culture while achieving success in all areas of our lives. Intellectual humility is a powerful tool that helps us navigate the vast sea of information and make meaningful contributions to our lives.

Breaking the Rhythm

In section A, we discovered how comfort zones can hold us back from fully experiencing life's vast potential. Living within these comfort zones may feel comfortable and predictable as the patterns are very rhythmic, but as time passes, we may start to feel dissatisfied and resentful. However, once we become aware of the tricks of logical fallacies that keep us stuck in these zones, we can break free from their patterns.

Comfort zones operate by using convincing logic. To break free from their hold, we must challenge the conventional thinking behind them. It means realizing that the logic used to justify staying in our comfort zones may not be as reasonable as it seems; instead, it serves the intention of avoiding discomfort. So, even if a logic appears rational, if its true purpose is to maintain comfort, it becomes disempowering and limiting. By recognizing this, we can liberate ourselves from the constraints of our comfort zones and open the door to new possibilities and growth.

One of the key ingredients is patience, that is required to figure out the nature and the extent of the logic in the comfort zone.

Step by step, let's learn how to break the rhythm:

- **Create Awareness**: Begin by becoming aware of your comfort zone. Take some time to reflect on areas of your life where you tend to feel secure and comfortable, but also notice if these areas might be limiting your growth and potential.
- **Identify the Kind of Comfort Zone**: Once you are aware of your comfort zone, identify what type it falls under - as discussed in section A. It could be related to knowledge, habits, physical spaces, beliefs, or other aspects of your life.
- **Recognize the Rhythm**: Next, observe the patterns and rhythms associated with your comfort zone. Notice how you tend to repeat certain behaviours or responses in those areas, and how it creates a sense of predictability.
- **Break the Rhythm**: To break free from the comfort zone's hold, challenge the familiar patterns. Try stepping outside your comfort zone in small, manageable ways. Take risks, try new experiences, and embrace uncertainty. In this manner, over time, you can liberate yourself from your comfort zone and become more adaptable to change.

Alex had big dreams and ambitious goals, but whenever he faced a challenging task, his comfort zone would step in like a cunning advisor. It would come up with all sorts of seemingly logical reasons to postpone the task, convincing him that it wasn't as difficult as he initially believed.

This pattern repeated itself every time, leading to a cycle of procrastination and delays. Little did Alex know that this comfortable path was slowly poisoning his progress. With each postponed task, the desired path slipped further away.

However, one day, a wise mentor came into his life and pointed out the flaw in his thinking. The mentor explained that the intention behind the logic presented by the comfort zone needed to be questioned. Was the intention just to remain in the comfort zone?

It was a tough realization for Alex, and he knew that breaking free from this cycle would require patience and determination. He had to learn to distinguish between genuine limitations and the deceptive whispers of the comfort zone.

The journey to break free from the comfort zone was extremely discomforting, as expected. But Alex understood that this discomfort was a sign of progress. Real change and growth often come with pain, just like a caterpillar transforming into a butterfly.

In time, Alex started to embrace the discomfort and challenges. He began to see his old self as the necessary stepping stone for the new self he was becoming. The old beliefs and habits were transformed into nutrients for his personal growth.

With each task faced head-on, Alex's confidence grew, and he found himself closer to his dreams. He had finally understood that escaping the fallacy of the comfort zone was the key to unlocking his true potential and living life to the fullest. And so, with newfound determination, Alex continued his journey towards greatness, ready to face any challenge that came his way.

Breaking the rhythm of your comfort zone will be uncomfortable at first, but it is a crucial step in personal growth and self-discovery. Embrace the process, be patient with yourself, and celebrate every small step towards breaking free from your comfort zone. As you gradually push the boundaries, you'll open up new opportunities for happiness, fulfillment, and success in life.

Time Mastery

Mastering time is a crucial aspect often overlooked by many individuals. In today's fast-paced world, despite its significance, people often fail to recognize the importance of utilizing the precious time available to them. In the current era, where resources abound and distractions are plentiful, the proper management of time has become even more critical. These resources encompass information, entertainment, hyperpalatable food, materialistic possessions, and emotional gratification. Throughout the day, we tend to spend a considerable amount of our precious time fulfilling our desires, which is necessary to a certain extent. However, with the advent of technology and its associated conveniences, many of us find ourselves with additional time at our disposal. If this surplus time is not utilized meaningfully, it will be consumed by the abundance of resources that surround us.

Sadly, overconsumption has become a pervasive issue in our lives, resulting in a host of mental, physical, and relationship problems. It can be viewed as a crime committed against oneself, as indulging in excess not only depletes our valuable time but also hinders personal growth and well-being. Consequently, it is essential to channel our time and energy towards endeavors that truly matter and bring us fulfillment.

By effectively managing our time, we can promote and nurture our creativity, a quality that often gets overlooked in the busyness of daily life. When we invest our precious time in meaningful activities, we create a space for innovation, self-expression, and personal development. Time mastery allows us to tap into our inherent potential, fostering a sense of purpose and accomplishment.

Moreover, effective time management enables us to strike a balance between various aspects of our lives. The concept of time mastery is multifaceted and requires a proactive approach. In the following segments, we will delve deeper into strategies and practices that can assist us in mastering time effectively and deriving the maximum benefit from this invaluable resource.

The Idea of Four Time Slots

Time is a precious resource that shapes our lives, and how we choose to spend it greatly impacts our overall well-being and pursuit of happiness. If we could organize our day into four special time slots, each dedicated to specific activities, that would help us maximize the use of our time. This concept of "Four Time Slots" can be a powerful framework to make the most of our available time and lead a more balanced and fulfilling life.

- **Morning Time**: The morning is a fresh start to the day, offering a wonderful opportunity to kickstart our day on an uplifting note. During this time, we can dedicate moments to activities that contribute to our personal growth and well-being. Engaging in exercises, journaling, or pursuing hobbies that ignite our passion and creativity can be incredibly beneficial. Investing in self-care during this time slot sets a rhythm for the rest of the day, enhancing our mental and physical well-being.
- **Office Time**: For many of us, work and other professional commitments are a significant part of our lives. Allocating specific time for office-related tasks allows us to be more focused and productive. During this slot, we can dedicate our energy to fulfilling work responsibilities, attending meetings, handling emails, upgrading professional skills and making progress on our professional goals. Effectively managing work-related tasks within this designated time allows us to create a rewarding professional life.
- **Evening Time**: As the day winds down, evenings provide a chance to relax and engage in activities that bring joy and fulfillment. Depending on individual preferences and priorities, evenings can be utilized for spending quality time with family and friends, pursuing hobbies, engaging in recreational activities, or simply enjoying some "me time." Allocating this slot for activities that align with our values and passions allows us to recharge, cultivate meaningful connections, and create a sense of balance in our lives. Proper utilization of this slot is essential for a fulfilling life.
- **Bedtime**: Prioritizing sufficient and restful sleep is crucial for our overall well-being and optimal functioning. Although in the order of the "four time slots" it comes at the end, it is the core of our 24 hour schedule. We need to fix our bedtime for an effective use of remaining slots. Establishing a bedtime routine that promotes relaxation and quality sleep ensures that we are physically and mentally rejuvenated for the next day. A good night's sleep is like hitting the reset button for our minds and bodies, setting us up for a fresh start in the morning.

It's important to recognize that while the concept of Four Time Slots offers a helpful framework, it's not a rigid structure. Life is dynamic, and our priorities may shift over time. The key is to be flexible and adaptable, making intentional choices to allocate time to activities that truly matter to us.

Through conscious time management and purposeful investments, we can optimize our daily routines, boost productivity, and make room for experiences that enhance our well-being. Adopting the concept of Four Time Slots empowers us to fully utilize our time and lead lives filled with fulfillment.

Time Management Tools

To make the most of our time in the four time slots, we can use some awesome tools to help us. These tools boost our time management skills and make life easier. Let's learn about them:

- **Planning**: It is drawing a map for our day. It means creating a plan with a detailed schedule and specific goals for each part of the day. When we know what we have to do and when, we can use our time better. Planning keeps us organized and helps us stay on course, so we don't waste time on things that don't matter or get sidetracked.

  To make planning even better, we can use tools like calendars, to-do lists, or time management apps. These tools remind us of important tasks, help us decide what's most important, and keep us focused on what we need to do.

- **Delegation**: It is having a team of helpers to share the work. Sometimes, there are tasks that others can do just as well, or even better, than us. By trusting capable people with specific responsibilities, we can save time and energy for more important tasks or activities that we are good at and enjoy doing.

  Effective delegation requires good communication and trust. We need to clearly explain what needs to be done and have confidence that the person we delegate to can handle the task. It's a great way to empower others and build stronger relationships, both in our work and personal life. At the same time, it's also an effective way to manage our time better.

- **Outsourcing**: It is getting expert help for certain tasks. There are times when we face tasks that are beyond our expertise or require specialized skills. Instead of struggling or spending too much time learning something new, we can hire professionals or use services that excel in those areas.

  For example, outsourcing might involve hiring a graphic designer for a project, getting a professional accountant for financial matters, or hiring a cleaning service to take care of household chores. This helps in ensuring high-quality results and saves valuable time and effort.

- **Parking**: It is hitting pause on non-urgent tasks. Not everything needs to be done immediately, and some tasks can wait until we have more time or energy to focus on them. By identifying tasks that are not time-sensitive and setting them aside for later, we prevent ourselves from feeling overwhelmed or stressed.

  Parking can involve using tools like reminder apps or sticky notes to jot down tasks we plan to do later. This way, we don't forget about them, and we can address them when we have the right time and mindset.

- **Renouncement**: It is letting go of things that don't truly matter. Many people unknowingly waste a lot of precious time doing unwanted things. Sometimes, we find ourselves committed to tasks, activities, or obligations that don't align with our priorities or bring significant value to our lives. It's essential to evaluate these commitments and be willing to say no or reduce our involvement in them. By renouncing these unnecessary things, we free ourselves to focus on what truly matters to us. It ensures that we have more time and energy for the activities and relationships that contribute to our happiness and personal growth.

By incorporating these time management tools into our routine, we can optimize the utilization of our time in the four slots. A combination of detailed planning, delegation, outsourcing, parking, and renouncement helps us filter out non-essential or less important tasks. This allows us to concentrate on meaningful and significant tasks that contribute to our personal growth, happiness, and productivity.

Furthermore, parallel working through delegation and outsourcing allows us to handle multiple tasks simultaneously when appropriate, multiplying the available time and enhancing efficiency.

Example: Here is an example of how time management tools can be applied in the regular activities of the kitchen, showcasing the effective utilisation of resources and maximising efficiency.

Let's delve into the numerous tasks involved in managing the kitchen efficiently.

- **Assessing procurement needs**: Identify the necessary ingredients and supplies required for cooking.
- **Procurement:** Acquiring the ingredients and supplies needed for meal preparation.
- **Cleaning and storage:** Ensuring a clean and organised kitchen space and appropriately storing ingredients and utensils.
- **Pre-cooking preparations:** Tasks such as cutting, boiling, or any preliminary steps needed before the actual cooking process.
- **Final cooking:** Executing the cooking process, bringing all the ingredients together to create delicious meals.
- **Serving:** Presenting the prepared dishes in an appealing manner for savoring and delight.
- **Winding up and utensil cleaning:** Cleaning and tidying up the kitchen, including washing utensils and maintaining a neat environment.

Breaking down kitchen tasks into specific categories is an essential part of effective planning in time management. By identifying and organising the various activities involved in meal preparation, individuals can create a structured plan that optimises their time and resources.

Once the planning phase for kitchen tasks is complete, it's time to leverage other time management tools like delegation, outsourcing, parking, and renouncement to ensure overall effectiveness.

Delegation can be employed in the kitchen by assigning specific tasks to other capable individuals. For example, family members or near ones can be delegated the responsibility of procurement, pre-cooking preparations, or even the final cooking process. By sharing the workload, individuals can focus on more critical aspects of meal preparation, maximising their productivity and efficiency.

Outsourcing certain kitchen tasks is another valuable tool. This could involve cleaning and storage, ordering pre-cut vegetables, ready-to-cook ingredients to save time on chopping and preparation or winding up and utensil cleaning. Alternatively, individuals can hire catering services or utilise meal delivery options for special occasions or busy days. Outsourcing allows individuals to benefit from specialised expertise and resources, reducing the burden of certain time-consuming tasks.

Parking becomes relevant in the kitchen when non-urgent tasks can be temporarily set aside to prioritise immediate needs. For example, if the final cooking stage requires undivided attention, a non-urgent incoming call can be parked for a later time. By focusing on the most time-sensitive tasks first, individuals can ensure that nothing gets overlooked or rushed.

Renouncement plays a role in the kitchen by letting go of non-essential tasks or commitments that may not align with the overall goal. This could involve skipping elaborate garnishes or complicated recipes that aren't necessary for the desired outcome. By renouncing unnecessary steps or excessive perfectionism, individuals can streamline their cooking process and save valuable time and energy.

By incorporating these time management tools into the identified kitchen tasks, individuals can optimise their time, streamline their workflow, and enhance their overall effectiveness in meal preparation.

Similarly, we can implement the concept of time mastery into our daily routines. By using the idea of four time slots, we can achieve greater control over our activities and enhance our efficiency. Let's explore how this approach can be applied for exam preparation as an example:

Phase 1: Strategic Planning

- Start by developing a thorough plan customized for the target. Evaluate the syllabus, required study materials, and allocate time for each subject.
- Identify areas that can be outsourced, such as study materials, live classes, video lectures, and test series.
- Recognize tasks that can be delegated, including household chores, meals, and certain study-related activities.
- Pinpoint activities that can be put on hold or parked, like indulging in movies, media consumption, and hyperpalatable foods.
- Identify habits and practices that need to be renounced for greater focus, such as excessive screen time, unproductive routines, and excessive idle periods.

Phase 2: Structured Planning

Create a detailed schedule applying the idea of four time slots.

- **Sleep Time Slot**: Start by setting a fixed sleep schedule to ensure enough rest. Determine your bedtime and wake-up time.
- **Morning Slot**: Allocate time for morning rituals, including refreshing activities and breakfast. Afterward, divide your available time into study sessions ranging from 1 to 1 hour 15 minutes, with short breaks of 15 to 30 minutes in between. Plan a longer break of around 2 hours at the end of this slot, including lunch.

- **Midday Slot**: After lunch break, follow a similar pattern with study sessions and breaks, just as in the morning. Allocate about 1 hour for a break at the end of this slot. Consider having dinner during this break.
- **Evening Slot**: Divide the evening hours into productive study sessions and intermediary breaks, adhering to the same structure as before. Dedicate 15 minutes for a quick review to assess the progress and compliance for the day. If any gap is found, plug it in the next day.

Each productive study session needs to be used according to the allocated time for each subject. More time should be allocated to subjects that require more attention.

By structuring our day into these distinct time slots and following a disciplined routine, we can master our use of time, enhance our productivity, and create a conducive environment for successful preparation. Managing our time will help us control our daily activities. This approach can improve our overall effectiveness and focus.

Effective time management is a dynamic process that requires regular evaluation, adjustments, and flexibility. By utilizing these time management tools and tailoring them to our specific needs and circumstances, we can make the most of our valuable time and create a more fulfilling and balanced life. Adopt these time management techniques and make each day count.

Revamping the Program

We explored the concept of "Unmasking the Identity" and "Constraints" in Section A. Now we understand the importance of self-awareness, understanding and our limitations due to conditioning. These insights are crucial in making meaningful changes and navigating our personal journeys with ease.

Our upbringing, environment, and experiences shape our thoughts, beliefs, and behaviours, which can sometimes create challenges in life. Recognizing the influence of these factors is a significant step towards personal growth and overcoming obstacles. We need to question and challenge beliefs and patterns that no longer serve us. This process helps us understand ourselves better and make choices that align with our values and aspirations.

One of the key ways to overcome our conditioning is through the power of repetition. This is all about rewiring our thoughts and behaviours. Regularly adopting new perspectives and behaviours gradually weakens the influence of long-held habits, opening pathways to renewed choices and possibilities. Just like a steady drip of water can wear away rock over time, repeating new patterns can reshape our minds. This process highlights the importance of persistence and patience, showing that gradual repetition can lead to profound change, freeing us from old limitations and letting us make conscious choices.

Let me share a profound shift that happened in my life when I delved into the topic of "Cruelty." It was a transformative journey that opened my eyes to the impact of our actions on others, whether intentional or unconscious. I realized that even unknowingly continuing harmful acts constituted cruelty. This realization was deeply connected to my introspective exercise of understanding "Unmasking the Identity".

My upbringing had instilled the consumption of animal products in me, yet I remained unaware of this influence until embarking on a journey of self-discovery. Through this process of personal realization, I challenged my conditioned beliefs actively and dedicated myself to change. After a year of unwavering commitment and practice, I can confidently state that I have chosen to adopt veganism, resulting in a complete transformation of my lifestyle.

One poignant experience that solidified my commitment to veganism was while watching a movie. I witnessed young children bravely rescuing animals just moments before their slaughter. This powerful scene reinforced my dedication to compassion and kindness, encouraging me to stay on the vegan path. While my initial motive was rooted in showing kindness towards animals, I discovered an unexpected benefit along the way. Adopting veganism opened up a whole new world of culinary possibilities. Previously, my food choices were limited, but now I am delighted to explore diverse and exciting food products that I never knew existed.

My relationship with food has transformed remarkably. It is no longer driven by default conditioning but by conscious and intentional design. This realization has taught me a valuable lesson: when we take charge of our lives and intentionally design them, it brings tremendous benefits. By questioning our ingrained beliefs and welcoming new possibilities, we unlock the potential for a more fulfilling and rewarding existence.

In my ongoing journey of redesigning life, I am now exploring other important areas of the intriguing world of human sexuality, an aspect that is highly misunderstood by most people. I have come to realize that this intricate part of our lives is not only shaped by our individual experiences and emotions but also heavily influenced by the conditioning of our environment. This is why it's crucial to redesign our lives, aiming to reduce the powerful influence of default conditioning.

Resilience

Resilience is a fundamental character trait that empowers us to navigate life's challenges with grace and strength. It helps us bounce back swiftly and effectively from tough times. When we encounter setbacks or adversities, resilient individuals possess a unique ability to adapt, learn, and grow from these experiences.

Imagine a person facing a significant setback in their career, such as losing their job unexpectedly. A resilient individual would not dwell on despair but instead, they would take proactive steps to cope and move forward. They might seek support from their network, update their resume, and actively search for new job opportunities. Instead of letting the setback define them, they use it as a stepping stone to new possibilities.

Resilience is not just limited to handling professional challenges; it is an integral part of emotional intelligence too. Emotionally intelligent individuals possess the mental fortitude to handle criticism and rejection without becoming overwhelmed or disheartened. Instead of getting discouraged, they use these experiences as opportunities for growth and learning.

Life is inherently unpredictable, filled with unforeseen events and obstacles. Resilience allows individuals to approach these situations with a flexible mindset. Rather than getting stuck or rigid in their ways, resilient individuals demonstrate an openness to change. They can adapt their plans and perspectives as needed, maintaining a sense of balance and stability even when facing adverse conditions.

To better grasp resilience, consider our default state as a relaxed and peaceful mind. However, external factors often disrupt this state, causing stress and tension. Resilience is the inclination and ability to return to a state of mental relaxation as quickly as possible after experiencing challenging circumstances. It involves finding ways to relax and regain our inner peace, even amidst adversity.

Emotional baggage and past experiences can weigh us down and hinder our ability to be resilient. Just as we discard physical garbage to maintain cleanliness and order, we must release the mental burdens that hold us back. Letting go of these emotional weights frees us to face challenges with a fresh perspective and renewed strength.

Moreover, resilience is not just about bouncing back from adversity; it involves self-reflection too. After regaining our normal mental state, the second part of resilience involves analyzing the causes that led to the challenging circumstances. This introspection helps us gain valuable insights and learn from our experiences, making us better equipped to navigate similar situations. It encourages personal growth, developing healthier ways of coping and dealing with difficulties, allowing us to thrive and grow even in the face of challenges. By embodying resilience, we become the heroes of our own stories, turning obstacles into opportunities for transformation.

Tia was fun loving, cheerful and her spirit radiated warmth and kindness. However, life had not always been gentle to her.

Tia's family faced numerous hardships. Her parents toiled tirelessly under the scorching sun, struggling to make ends meet. Yet, despite their daily struggles, they showered Tia with love and instilled in her the values of resilience and perseverance.

As Tia grew older, she encountered her own share of tribulations. At the tender age of ten, she was diagnosed with a rare and debilitating illness that left her frail and confined to a wheelchair. Suddenly, her world turned upside down. The vibrant colours of life seemed to fade, replaced by the somber shades of adversity.

But Tia refused to surrender to despair. Her spirit burned bright, fueled by a strong determination to overcome her circumstances. She found solace in books, immersing herself in tales of courage and triumph. These stories became her companions, inspiring her to believe in the power of resilience.

Tia's resilience faced a severe test when tragedy struck her village. A devastating storm ravaged the land, leaving destruction in its wake. Houses crumbled, fields were flooded, and the villagers were left broken and desperate. Tia's family, too, lost their home and all their belongings.

In the midst of this chaos, Tia's resilience shone like a beacon of hope. Despite her own physical limitations, she dedicated herself to helping others. She rallied her fellow villagers, encouraging them to rebuild their homes. With persistent determination, she organized relief efforts, providing food, shelter, and comfort to those in need.

Tia's story resonated far beyond the village, attracting people from distant lands. The tale of her resilience and compassion reached the ears of a renowned philanthropist named Mr. Samy. Deeply moved by Tia's extraordinary spirit, he pledged to support her in any way he could.

With Mr. Samy's assistance, Tia's village began to rise from the ashes. The once-shattered houses were restored, and the fields flourished with new life. But the true marvel lay in the transformation that had occurred within the villagers. Tia's resilience had not only rebuilt their homes but had also reignited their hope and ignited their own spirits of resilience.

As Tia witnessed her village thrive once more, she came to understand that resilience was not merely a personal attribute but a contagious force capable of uplifting an entire community. She realized that even in the darkest of times, when life seemed insurmountable, resilience possessed the power to mend shattered dreams and forge new paths of possibility.

Tia continues to inspire generations to come. She became a symbol of hope, reminding everyone that within each of us lies the strength to rise above adversity. Her journey taught us that resilience is not defined by physical abilities or material possessions but by the belief that we can overcome any obstacle life throws our way.

Psychological Resolution

Let's understand and practice the fascinating concept of psychological resolution. This idea is about finding a sense of completion or settlement to emotional events or conflicts in our lives. It's that feeling of contentment or finality we seek, which allows us to move forward and let go of emotional ties that might be holding us back.

In today's fast-paced world, where we often face information overload and a cluttered mind, psychological resolution can be a powerful tool to find inner peace and ease emotional distress. To achieve this, we can use affirmations and visualizations as helpful allies.

Affirmations are empowered statements we repeat to ourselves, like "I am seeking clarity and resolution within myself" or "I am finding resolution and peace within." By consciously affirming our intention to let go of burdensome thoughts and experiences, we open the door to transformative change.

Visualizations are also essential. We can create a mental space where we sort through our thoughts, symbolically organizing and releasing what no longer serves us. This process brings clarity and order to our minds, leading to settlement and resolution.

Acceptance, understanding, and a willingness to let go allows us to actively find resolution and bring calmness to our minds. Gradually, we can ease the burdens of emotional distress and cultivate a sense of inner peace.

The concept of psychological resolution is not limited to one area of life; it has significance in various aspects where unresolved emotions can impact our well-being. Whether it's overcoming past traumas, letting go of regrets, or finding resolution in relationships, practicing psychological resolution can guide us towards personal growth and a more fulfilling life.

This is a deeply personal journey, and it may take time. Be patient and kind to yourself throughout the process. By seeking resolution, we empower ourselves to live more freely and fully, unburdened by the weight of emotional baggage.

Here are some key areas where psychological resolution can be particularly relevant:

- **Grief and Loss:** The death of a loved one or the end of a significant relationship can leave us grappling with profound grief and a range of emotions. Finding resolution in these situations can help us process our feelings, accept the reality of the loss, and move forward while honouring the memory of what was lost.
- **Traumatic Experiences:** Individuals who have experienced trauma may struggle with lingering emotional wounds. Seeking resolution allows them to confront and make sense of their experiences, fostering healing.
- **Past Mistakes or Regrets:** Unresolved guilt, shame, or regret from past mistakes can weigh heavily on our minds, impacting our self-esteem and overall well-being. Psychological resolution enables us to learn from our mistakes and forgive ourselves.

- **End of a Chapter or Transition:** Resolution is often relevant when we reach the end of a significant chapter in our lives, such as completing a long-term project or leaving a job. It helps us acknowledge the journey, celebrate accomplishments, and prepare mentally and emotionally for what lies ahead.
- **Unresolved Relationships:** Relationships that end on a sour note or lack resolution can leave lingering feelings of resentment, hurt, or unfinished business. Seeking resolution in these relationships allows us to let go, heal emotional wounds, and create space for healthier connections.
- **Unmet Expectations:** When our expectations go unfulfilled, it can lead to feelings of disappointment and a sense of incompleteness. Psychological resolution helps us reframe our expectations, find meaning in the experience, and pursue new paths.

It is important to note that while psychological resolution is relevant in these areas, the process and timeline for finding resolution can vary for each individual. Engaging in self-reflection, and utilising various coping strategies can assist in the journey towards resolution and emotional well-being.

These two tales of Rajan and Meera will help us understand the practical benefits of this concept.

Rajan stood out for his insatiable thirst for wisdom and his relentless pursuit of inner transformation in the enchanting town of Panaji, where whispers of thrill and curiosity filled the air.

But life had not always been gentle to Rajan. He had faced numerous hardships that left scars on his inner self. The weight of unresolved emotions and painful memories burdened him, making it difficult for him to find peace within himself. He yearned to find a way to heal from the wounds of his past and seek resolution for the pain that lingered.

One fine day, while strolling through the cobbled streets, Rajan's attention was captivated by the weathered facade of an ancient bookstore. The old sign creaked gently in the breeze, inviting him inside. As he stepped through the creaking door, the smell of musty pages filled the air, drawing him deeper into the bookstore.

Rajan wandered through the shelves, his fingers gently caressing the spines of dusty tomes. Suddenly, a book caught his eye, its cover faded and its pages yellowed with age. The title read, "The Journey to inner peace".

Intrigued, Rajan took the book in his hands and sat down in a cozy corner of the bookstore. As he began to read, he felt an immediate connection to the words on the page. It was as if the book had been written specifically for him.

In the story, he met a character named Maya, who bore an uncanny resemblance to himself. Maya had experienced her fair share of hardships and emotional turmoil, much like Rajan. As he followed her journey through the pages, he saw himself reflected in her struggles and her relentless pursuit of resolution and inner peace.

As the days passed, Rajan became deeply engrossed in the book, finding solace in its words and wisdom. He couldn't help but wonder if he, too, could find the resolution he so desperately sought. He yearned to let go of the emotional burdens that weighed heavily on him and find a sense of completeness within himself.

One evening, as the sun dipped below the horizon, Rajan found himself lost in thought, contemplating the book's teachings. Suddenly, a gentle voice broke through his reverie, and he looked up to find an elderly man sitting across from him. The man's eyes twinkled with wisdom and kindness.

"Lost in the pages of a good book, are you?" the man said with a warm smile.

Rajan nodded, a hint of curiosity in his eyes. "Yes, this book has touched me in ways I cannot explain. It speaks of psychological resolution and finding inner peace".

The man's smile grew wider. "Ah, psychological resolution, a journey that many embark upon. It is a path of self-discovery. Tell me, young one, what do you seek in this quest for resolution?"

With a mixture of hesitation and vulnerability, Rajan opened up to the stranger. He shared his struggles and desires, his yearning to untangle the knots of unresolved emotions that burdened him.

The elderly man listened intently, nodding empathetically. "To find resolution, one must delve deep into their own mind," he said. "It is a journey of self-reflection and forgiveness, a process of letting go of what no longer serves us."

Rajan felt a sense of comfort in the man's words. "But how do I begin this journey?" he asked, feeling a mix of hope and uncertainty.

The wise man leaned in closer, his voice soft and reassuring. "Start by accepting that resolution is a gradual process. Be kind to yourself and allow yourself the time to heal. Explore your emotions and memories, understanding that they are part of what makes you who you are".

As the evening turned to night, Rajan and the wise man engaged in a role play of sorts, where they took turns stepping into the shoes of different characters from the book. They acted out scenarios of finding resolution, each moment carrying a profound message of healing and growth.

Through the role play, Rajan gained a deeper understanding of the principles of psychological resolution. He saw how forgiveness and understanding could lead to the unburdening of the self and the discovery of inner peace.

In the following days, Rajan continued to explore the book's teachings and engage in conversations with the wise man. With each passing moment, he felt a sense of transformation taking root within him. He started the process of self-discovery, knowing that he was on the path to healing and resolution.

And so, the story of Rajan serves as a reminder to all that within each of us lies the strength to rise above adversity, to find resolution, and to tread the journey of self-discovery with courage and hope.

Meera was brimming with kindness and compassion, and she brought comfort to everyone she encountered. But beneath her warm exterior, Meera carried a burden of sorrow that weighed heavily on her spirit. It was the loss of her parents at a tender age that left a void in her, making her feel incomplete.

Amidst the tranquility of the town of Manali, Meera found solace in her grandmother, Charu, who became her pillar of strength and guidance. Charu's love and wisdom encased Meera like a warm blanket, filling the void left by her parents. She was not just a grandmother, she was a guardian angel, guiding Meera through life's trials and teaching her the values of compassion and inner strength.

But Charu's time with Meera was limited. The day she bid her farewell, the world seemed to lose its brilliance, and Meera was shrouded in grief and longing. The pain of losing her grandmother left her grappling for resolution– a way to find peace amidst the storm of emotions. She remembered the teaching of Charu about the significance of psychological resolution in such a situation.

Meera embarked on a profound journey of healing. She delved into the teachings of some contemporary books, eager to understand the path towards inner peace. Her quest was not just about finding a way to forget the pain but about honoring the love she had shared with Charu and finding a way to carry her memory with grace.

In her pursuit of resolution, Meera engaged in heartfelt conversations with her closest friends. She poured out her feelings, shared cherished memories of Charu, and allowed herself to be vulnerable. Through these conversations, she found a cathartic release, as if the weight of her grief was shared and lightened.

To honor her grandmother's legacy, Meera took to writing. In a journal adorned with delicate patterns, she penned down their beautiful journey together, capturing every precious moment they had shared. Each stroke of her pen became a testament to their bond, and with each word, Meera felt a sense of resolution growing within her.

Nature became Meera's sanctuary. She would visit the places where she and Charu had spent precious moments – a serene garden filled with colourful blooms or a quiet lakeside bench where they would converse for hours. Surrounded by the beauty of nature, Meera felt her grandmother's presence, and it brought comfort to her.

As Meera continued her journey of healing, she realized that resolution was not a sudden end to her grief but a gentle transition. The memories of her grandmother were etched in her mind forever, and they had become a cherished part of her being. The ache of loss transformed into a bittersweet reminder of the love they had shared, a love that would always remain alive within her.

Through her journey, Meera taught the town of Manali the power of healing and remembrance. She proved that resolution was not about erasing the past but about finding a way to honor our experiences and navigate through grief with grace and understanding. Meera's story became a reminder that the love we share with our near ones never truly fades, and by preserving their memory, we find the strength to create a new chapter of healing and growth.

The importance of psychological resolution cannot be underestimated, as it deeply influences our emotional well-being and personal development. When we process through psychological resolution, we acknowledge and process our emotions fully. By facing any pain, grief, or anger within us, we begin the process of healing. It helps us understand and accept the experiences that have shaped us.

Resolution also allows us to let go of burdens that weigh us down. We can release regrets, resentments, and attachments that hinder our growth and prevent us from living in the present moment. This newfound freedom empowers us to forgive ourselves and others, leading to a sense of liberation.

The impact of psychological resolution extends beyond ourselves; it has a constructive influence on our relationships with others. When we achieve resolution, we can approach connections with empathy, compassion, and understanding. This enables us to form healthier and more fulfilling relationships.

Exploration

Exploration is a key aspect of our journey towards happiness and fulfillment. While we strive to achieve success in our lives, it's essential to recognize the value of exploration. For those of us who have the privilege of having enough resources to meet our basic needs, exploration opens up a world of possibilities.

The pursuit of happiness depends on the expansion of our lives; through exploration, we gain a substantial amount of expansion. Most of us are unaware of this aspect of life, leading us to confine ourselves within various comfort zones that impede expansion. Such a lifestyle will diminish the quality of our lives, rendering them uninteresting. On the other hand, if we recognize the importance of exploration, we can experience significant expansion in our words, actions, and thoughts, thereby making our life more engaging and joyful. Here is an example that illustrates how expansion operates: modern shopping malls often feature high ceilings, so upon entering such a building, we experience a sense of elevation due to their contrast with regular buildings that have lower ceilings. These temporary elevated feelings also influence our spending behaviour, causing us to suddenly spend more.

Let's consider another example from our daily routine: when we wake up in the morning, being confined within a room or house restricts us from experiencing expansion. The moment we step out to open air, we experience a sudden sense of expansion and an elevated feeling. We can encounter this type of expansion every day; these small moments can signal the beginning of our exploration journey. This heightened sensation is what we mean by expansion. Understanding its significance and its connection to lasting happiness is essential for incorporating exploration into our lives.

In today's technologically advanced world, we have access to a wealth of information and opportunities. Unlike previous generations, we can explore and dive deep into areas that ignite our curiosity and passion. This is a treasure trove of knowledge and experiences at our fingertips.

Why is exploration more relevant, in the contemporary world? Well, the truth is that excessive consumption can take a toll on our well-being. We may find ourselves feeling overwhelmed, stressed, and disconnected from what truly matters. That's where exploration comes in as a remedy.

Instead of getting caught up in the never-ending cycle of consuming, we can channel our surplus energy and time into exploration. Think of it as embarking on a journey of self-discovery and growth. We can explore various hobbies, interests, and activities that light us up and bring us joy.

Perhaps you've always wanted to learn a new skill, like playing a musical instrument or painting. Or maybe you've been curious about different cultures and want to travel and experience the world. With the resources at our disposal, the possibilities are endless.

Exploration also enriches our relationships. By exploring new experiences together with our near ones, we create lasting memories and strengthen our bonds. It's a chance to connect on a deeper level and share the joy of discovery. The beauty of exploration is that it can be tailored to our unique interests and passions. It could be as simple as trying out a new recipe, reading books on topics that intrigue us, or attending workshops to expand our knowledge.

Let's take the time to reflect on what truly sparks our curiosity and brings us a sense of fulfillment. Once we have an idea, let's start exploring with an open mind and an adventurous spirit. There may be challenges along the way, but each experience will be a valuable stepping stone on our path to personal growth and happiness.

As we explore, we need to be kind to ourselves. It's not about achieving perfection or mastering every new skill. It's about the journey, the process of learning, and the joy of discovery. Enjoy the excitement of the unknown, and let exploration lead us to new horizons and a more enriched and meaningful life.

In our journey of exploration, there are numerous techniques that we can delve into, and I have some wonderful suggestions. Let's divide our exploration into two parts: life skills and life management.

Setting foot on the path of life skills discovery unveils a vast landscape of mental and physical well-being. From exploring our thoughts, emotions, and relationships to enhancing air quality and adopting healthy habits, this journey encompasses diverse domains. Moreover, immersing ourselves in creative outlets like music, dance, writing, and culinary arts enriches our existence. Transitioning to life management, we learn to navigate stress, address habits, and confront substance abuse, all while mastering the art of time and resource allocation. This holistic exploration promises a more enlightened and balanced way of living.

Part 1 - Life Skills

- **Mental Health**
    - **Psychology**: Exploring areas of psychology like cognitive, developmental, educational, social, organisational/industrial, health, and neuropsychology provides insights into human behaviour, learning, relationships, and well-being. This exploration not only informs practical applications in education, mental health, and workplace dynamics but also has a good impact on our overall well-being. By gaining a deeper understanding of ourselves and others, we can implement effective interventions and strategies, contributing to our personal growth.
    - **Terrestrial Exploration**: Exploring the surroundings offers a magnificent avenue for broadening our thoughts and perspectives, enabling us to delve deeper into the world around us.
    - **Resource Exploration**: The abundance of natural and man-made resources bestowed upon us provides an extraordinary opportunity to uncover and harness their immense potential for the benefit of our lives. Since it is part of our lives we hardly notice it. Conscious exploration of these resources gives a new dimension to our thinking process.
    - **Beliefs and Practices**: Embarking on an insightful journey of exploration, we can delve deeply into various beliefs and practices,

seeking to comprehend their profound connection with human beings.

- **Stressors**: Exploring sources of stress to improve mental and emotional well-being.
- **Obsessive Habits**: Exploring unhealthy obsessions and habits to promote a balanced lifestyle.
- **Substance Abuse**: Gaining knowledge about the causes and consequences of substance abuse and exploring ways to overcome it.

- **Physical Health**
    - **Primary Need**: Air: Exploring the importance of clean air and ways to improve indoor and outdoor air quality.
    - **Food and Digestion**: Understanding the impact of food on the body and exploring healthy eating habits.
    - **Cleanliness**: Exploring the significance of cleanliness in maintaining a hygienic and organised living environment.
    - **Sleep**: Exploring the importance of quality sleep and exploring ways to improve sleep patterns and habits.
- **Other Skills**
    - **Music**: Exploration of music as a skill opens doors to new perspectives, expanding our thoughts and horizons in captivating ways.
    - **Dance**: Exploring the realm of dance paves the way for new pathways to unfold, enriching our lives in countless dimensions.
    - **Writing**: Exploring the realm of writing not only nurtures refined thinking patterns but also unveils unexplored realms of knowledge.
    - **Culinary**: Food, an essential component of our existence, provides a realm ripe with possibilities for exploration. Investing time, energy, and resources to explore the art of cooking opens up meaningful avenues for self-expression and creativity.

Part 2 - Life Management

- **Home Front**
  - **Spousal Relationship**: Engaging in exploration of open communication, active listening, and exploring new ways to strengthen emotional intimacy and connection with one's partner.
  - **Parenting**: Continuously learning and exploring various approaches to nurture children's development, understanding their individual needs, and fostering a loving and supportive environment for their growth.
  - **Elderly Care**: Exploring compassionate caregiving techniques, seeking knowledge about aging-related issues, and finding innovative ways to enhance the quality of life for elderly family members.
  - **Kitchen Management:** Exploring new kitchen skills, experimenting with diverse kitchen management techniques and incorporating healthy and sustainable practices into daily food preparation and meal planning.
  - **Gardening**: Delving into the world of plants, exploring different gardening techniques, experimenting with various types of plants and landscaping, and discovering the therapeutic benefits of connecting with nature.
  - **Housekeeping**: Exploring efficient and eco-friendly cleaning methods, organising systems, and decluttering techniques to maintain a clean, tidy, and harmonious living space.
  - **Financial Management**: Engaging in financial literacy, exploring sensible expenditure, investment opportunities, budgeting techniques, and exploring sustainable practices to maximize savings and achieve long-term financial goals.

- **Professional Front**
  - **Learning New Skills**: Cultivating a mindset of continuous learning, exploring various educational resources, and expanding one's knowledge and expertise in diverse areas of interest.
  - **Handling Behaviour**: Developing emotional intelligence, exploring effective communication strategies, and learning techniques for managing challenging behaviours in oneself and others.
  - **Relationship Management:** Nurturing healthy and meaningful connections with others, exploring effective conflict resolution strategies, and seeking personal growth through congenial relationships.
  - **Professional Ethics**: Explore professional ethics by reflecting on personal values, ethical frameworks, and aligning actions with professional responsibility.
  - **Handling Workplace Stress**: Exploring stress management techniques, practicing self-care, and seeking support and resources to effectively navigate workplace stressors and maintain overall well-being.

Exploration is an incredible journey that plays a vital role in our lives. Nowadays, we have unprecedented access to vast amounts of information, making exploration easier and more exciting. With dedication and curiosity, we can delve into any subject that piques our interest and embark on a quest to uncover new knowledge and understanding. The beauty of exploration lies in its ability to expand our horizons and challenge our existing beliefs, contributing to a deeper understanding of the world around us.

What's even more fantastic is that we can share our exploration findings with others. By documenting our experiences, insights, and discoveries, we can inspire and enlighten a broader audience. Whether through books, content creation, or engaging discussions, we have the power to encourage others to embark on their own exploration journeys.

Exploration isn't just about gaining knowledge; it's also a journey of personal growth and self-discovery. As we immerse ourselves in new subjects, we uncover fresh perspectives, acquire valuable skills, and learn more about ourselves. The process of exploration challenges our intellect and curiosity, giving us a sense of fulfillment and achievement.

Beyond personal growth, exploration drives innovation and progress. Countless groundbreaking discoveries and advancements have been made through dedicated exploration. By pushing the boundaries of what we know, we can find solutions to complex problems and make significant breakthroughs.

Embrace the Inner Majesty

Allow the Child to Play and Engage Youth in Creativity

Embracing the Inner Majesty is all about rediscovering the joy and creativity that lies within us, just like when we were children. Unlocking a treasure trove of happiness and boundless imagination can enrich our lives in beautiful ways.

When we allow the child within us to play, we give ourselves the freedom to be carefree and spontaneous. Remember those days when we laughed without any worries and explored the world with curiosity? By embracing our playful side, we can experience that joy again. It could be as simple as playing games, dancing to our favorite music, or spending time in nature, letting go of our adult responsibilities for a moment.

Alongside embracing playfulness, we must also tap into the creative spirit of our youth. As youngsters, we were full of imagination and creativity, dreaming big and daring to think differently. But as we grow up, sometimes we stifle that creative spark due to societal norms or fear of failure. Embracing the youth within us means unlocking that creativity once again, allowing ourselves to explore new ideas, take risks, and express ourselves freely through art, writing, or any other creative outlet.

By integrating playfulness and creativity, we create a beautiful harmony in our lives. Playfulness keeps us light-hearted and reminds us to find joy in the little things. On the other hand, creativity empowers us to innovate, discharge responsibility, solve problems, and embrace our unique talents.

Recognizing the Inner Majesty is not just about having fun and being creative for the sake of it. It has profound benefits for our well-being and personal growth. When we allow ourselves to play and explore our creativity, we reduce stress, boost our mood, and increase our sense of self-worth. We become more adaptable, open-minded and ready to face life's challenges.

Let's make time for playfulness and creativity in our daily lives. Engage in activities that make us happy and let our imagination run wild. Whether it's painting, writing, singing, or trying something completely new, let's embrace the childlike wonder and the boundless creativity of our youth. By taking such actions, we can embrace a life brimming with happiness, fulfillment, and boundless possibilities.

Ashok embarked on a heartfelt journey to bring back the joy and energy of his younger days. He realized that cherishing every moment and managing his time wisely could make a significant difference in his life.

Ashok's mornings became a special time for personal growth and reflection. Rising early, he engaged in activities that filled him with happiness and nourished his creativity. Whether it was pursuing a hobby, or reading inspiring books, he knew that starting the day with enthusiasm was crucial.

During his office hours, Ashok made the most of his time by using time management tools. He learned to prioritize his tasks and break them into smaller, manageable parts. This approach allowed him to be more productive and creative, finding a state of flow where he was fully absorbed in his work.

In the evenings, Ashok enjoyed playful moments with his family. He planned spontaneous outings, played games, and took leisurely walks, savoring the simple joys of life. These precious moments brought him closer to his loved ones and rekindled the carefree spirit of his inner child.

Before bedtime, Ashok understood the importance of winding down and preparing for a restful sleep. He practiced relaxation techniques, clearing his mind and reflecting on the day's experiences. This practice helped him wake up each day with renewed energy and enthusiasm.

Throughout his journey, Ashok realized that time management was the key to infusing his life with playfulness and youthful energy. By planning ahead, delegating tasks, and making time for self-expression and personal growth, he could fully immerse himself in the present moment.

Ashok's life taught us that it is never too late to rediscover the playfulness of childhood and the exuberance of youth. With a thoughtful approach and a playful spirit, we can make each moment count and fill our lives with boundless joy and creativity.

Respecting the Gender Wise Prominence of Child/youth

In the journey of life, we all carry the essence of both the child and the youth within us. When we consider gender, we can observe that certain child-like qualities are little more prominent in females, while the energy of youth is slightly more prominent in males. However, it's important to understand that these qualities are not exclusive to one gender or absent in the other; they simply vary in degrees of prominence.

To lead a fulfilling and happy life, we must value these prominences in the relationship between males and females. The key lies in mutual respect and appreciation. Males should respect the child-like innocence and playfulness within females, while females should appreciate the energetic and youthful qualities within males. We should acknowledge, respect, and learn from the natural prominence that each gender possesses.

By adopting this perspective, males can imbibe playfulness by observing the joy and lightheartedness of females. Similarly, females can find inspiration in the vibrant energy and enthusiasm displayed by males. This mutual respect and learning from one another create a harmonious balance in relationships, allowing both genders to grow and evolve together.

Recognizing and honoring the unique qualities within each gender fosters a deeper understanding and appreciation for one another. It promotes a sense of unity, respect, and synergy, leading to a more fulfilling and joyful life. By respecting the gender wise prominence of child/youth within us, we can create a place where all individuals are celebrated for their inherent qualities, contributing to a more harmonious and loving environment.

Nitu and Yash's tale blossomed over several years. They shared a deep bond and a unique understanding of each other, realizing the significance of embracing the child and youth within themselves and their relationship.

Nitu, with her nurturing and caring nature, radiated an aura of child-like innocence and playfulness. Her laughter was infectious, and her ability to find joy in the simplest of things was truly remarkable. She overflowed with compassion, and her caring nature brought comfort and warmth to those around her.

Yash, on the other hand, was a bundle of youthful energy and enthusiasm. He approached life with a vibrant spirit, seeking adventure and new experiences at every turn. His zest for life was contagious, and he inspired those around him to embrace the present moment and live life to the fullest.

At the beginning of their relationship, Nitu and Yash were intrigued by each other's unique qualities. Nitu admired Yash's ability to infuse every moment with excitement and his fearlessness in pursuing his dreams. Yash, in turn, was captivated by Nitu's ability to find joy in the little things and her nurturing nature that made their relationship feel like a safe haven.

As their understanding deepened, Nitu and Yash began to learn from each other's qualities. Nitu encouraged Yash to tap into his inner child, reminding him to find joy in the present and appreciate life's simple pleasures. Yash, in turn, encouraged Nitu to step out of her comfort zone and embrace her own youthful energy. They became each other's cheerleaders, supporting one another in their pursuit of personal growth and self-discovery.

Together, they embarked on new adventures, exploring various hobbies and activities that brought out their inner child and youth. They went on spontaneous trips, tried out different cuisines, and danced under the stars. Their lives became a delightful canvas of playfulness and excitement, with each day a new opportunity to cherish and celebrate life.

Nitu and Yash's journey together revealed the beauty of embracing the child and youth within themselves and each other. They found harmony in their relationship, supporting each other's growth and a sense of adventure. Their love thrived on playfulness and a deep connection, adding vibrancy and joy to their lives. By celebrating their unique qualities, they created a fulfilling and meaningful bond, reminding us of the importance of embracing our inner child and youthful spirit for a joyful and purposeful life.

Strategic Role Adaptation

When it comes to fulfilling the different roles we play in our lives, there are some smart strategies we can use to make things easier and more satisfying. These strategies help us handle the responsibilities and challenges that come with our roles in a more effective way.

Firstly, self-awareness and self-care are crucial. Knowing our own needs, values, and limits helps us set realistic expectations and boundaries in our roles. Taking care of our physical and mental well-being allows us to keep a healthy balance and approach our responsibilities with a clear and focused mind.

Another important strategy is effective communication. It's vital to express our needs, concerns, and boundaries clearly to those involved in our roles. When we listen actively and have open dialogues, we build better connections and solve conflicts more successfully, making our interactions smoother.

Flexibility and adaptability are also key strategies. We need to understand that circumstances and expectations can change, so being open to adjusting our approaches and finding creative solutions is essential. Being adaptable allows us to handle unexpected situations, overcome challenges, and maintain good relationships with others.

Being assertive is a valuable strategy in managing our social roles. By communicating our needs confidently and respectfully, we can navigate our responsibilities with more clarity, build self-confidence, and have healthier relationships with others.

One powerful strategy is role-playing. This means putting ourselves in someone else's shoes or adopting a specific role to better understand their perspective, needs, and expectations. Role-playing helps us develop empathy, improve communication skills, and find solutions to challenges that may arise in those roles.

In personal relationships, role-playing can help us handle difficult conversations and conflicts by seeing things from the other person's point of view.

Role-playing also offers room for self-reflection and growth. It allows us to look at our own behaviour and reactions in a certain role, identify areas where we can improve, and refine our approach. By stepping out of our own perspective, we gain a deeper understanding of the complexities involved in fulfilling our roles.

However, it's important to know that role-playing should be done with sensitivity, respect, and a genuine desire to understand and improve. It's not about pretending or manipulating, but about gaining insight to navigate our roles more effectively.

The Art of Losing Gracefully

In our journey towards happiness and peace, knowing how to lose gracefully during arguments is essential. It's not about giving up or suppressing our beliefs, but rather about showing humility, empathy, and effective communication. By approaching disagreements with understanding and respect, we can create harmony and personal growth.

Losing gracefully can be tough, especially in challenging scenarios when facing strong and confident logic, dealing with someone who seems foolish, handling emotionally manipulative people, or participating in a heated debate. Here are a few suggestions to navigate better in such situations.

Mastering Graceful Concessions in Challenging Argument Scenarios

- **Facing Strong Logic**: When someone presents strong and confident logic, it's crucial to keep an open mind and consider their viewpoint. Instead of getting defensive, acknowledge the strength of their reasoning and evidence. Find common ground and areas of agreement while still holding onto your own beliefs. Losing an argument doesn't mean you've failed personally; it can lead to growth and new perspectives.
- **Dealing with Foolishness**: Encountering someone who appears foolish or lacks logical reasoning can be frustrating. Instead of belittling them, practice empathy and patience. Understand their motives and concerns. Listen actively and ask questions to guide the conversation towards more constructive paths. Respectfully challenge their viewpoints while avoiding personal attacks.
- **Handling Emotional Manipulation**: When faced with emotional manipulation, it's essential to stay composed. Recognize tactics like guilt-tripping or emotional appeals, so as not to be entirely swayed by them. Focus on the actual points being discussed, relying on logic and evidence. Avoid being carried away by emotional appeals and bring the conversation back to rational reasoning and facts.
- **Managing Campaign-Style Arguments**: In a campaign-style argument, participants often come into the discussion with preconceived ideas or viewpoints that they aim to defend and promote. These preconceived ideas are typically aligned with their personal beliefs or interests. Engaging in a campaign-style argument can feel overwhelming, as it often prioritizes persuasive tactics over substantive discussion. Stay calm and focused on the issues at hand. Avoid personal attacks or getting caught up in theatrics. Point out logical fallacies

or inconsistencies in their arguments. Encourage a more meaningful exchange of ideas grounded in rationality.

Adopting humility and effective communication opens us to new perspectives and insights that contribute to our development. Losing gracefully isn't a sign of weakness but shows emotional intelligence and prioritizes personal growth and happiness. This approach creates an environment for well-being, fosters meaningful interactions, and enhances our overall happiness and personal growth.

Consistency

The saying "**We become what we repeatedly do**" holds a profound truth that highlights the cumulative effect of our habits and actions on who we are as individuals. As we explore various happiness pathfinders, it's natural to have doubts about how easily the presented concepts can be put into practice. At the beginning, they might appear challenging, but they can become ingrained in our lives with consistent effort and the cumulative effect of repetition, which we have discussed in section A under "subliminal storyline".

To illustrate the power of the cumulative effect, let's take a closer look at the journey of a guitar maestro. They achieve such skill and finesse not through a single practice session, but through hours upon hours of repeated strumming, fingerpicking, and mastering complex techniques. Over time, these small increments of practice create a cumulative effect, forming strong neural connections in their brain. As a result, playing the guitar becomes almost automatic and effortless.

Similarly, think about athletes who achieve greatness in their respective sports. It's not just a single moment of brilliance that makes them exceptional; it's the cumulative effect of consistent practice, training, and refinement of their skills over time.

In our own lives, the principle of repetition and its cumulative effect remains a powerful tool. If we want to learn a new language, the more consistently we practice speaking, reading, and writing in that language, the more we'll see the cumulative effect of our efforts. Our brain adapts to the language's patterns and nuances, making it easier to communicate fluently as time goes on.

The same principle applies to adopting empowering habits or changing disempowering ones. Whether it's becoming more organized, cultivating a healthier lifestyle, or developing a growth mindset, the cumulative effect of repeating these behaviours consistently leads to transformation and personal growth.

Good time management is crucial in achieving this cumulative effect. By allocating dedicated time each day to practice and work on our goals, we harness the power of consistency and build momentum towards our aspirations.

I want to emphasize the profound effect the techniques suggested in happiness pathfinders can have on our lives through the principle of repetition. Consistently applying these strategies, day after day, allows them to take root in our minds and behaviour, leading to meaningful and lasting changes that contribute to our overall happiness and well-being. Practice and repetition are the keys to unlocking the true power of these techniques and experiencing transformative results in our lives.

Chapter 12

EVALUATION

When we consistently incorporate the suggested pathfinders into our daily lives, we can anticipate effective outcomes. These pathfinders are guiding principles that lead us towards personal growth and improved self-esteem. By following them with dedication and perseverance, we set ourselves on a journey of self-discovery and self-improvement.

The "Self Esteem measurement parameters-Score sheet" in section A provides a valuable tool to gauge the effectiveness of these practices. This score sheet acts as a self-assessment tool, allowing us to reflect on our progress and understand how the pathfinders are influencing our self-esteem. By evaluating our experiences and feelings using the score sheet, we gain insights into the impact of these practices on our overall well-being.

As we use the score sheet regularly, we can observe how our self-esteem scores change over time. It enables us to identify patterns and trends, showing us which pathfinders have the most significant impact on our self-esteem. By paying attention to these results, we can adjust our approach and focus on the pathfinders that bring about the most empowering changes in our lives.

The process of using the score sheet and assessing our progress helps us stay committed to the journey of self-improvement. It acts as a source of accountability, reminding us to stay consistent with the pathfinders and reminding us of the importance of nurturing our self-esteem.

With each small improvement in our self-esteem, we build a foundation of confidence and self-assurance that permeates every aspect of our lives.

END NOTE

We need to become smart investors, investing our time, energy, and resources to ensure maximum profit through harvesting the **Low hanging fruit in the garden of life.**

"Happiness is the ultimate wealth, surpassing all material possessions, as it brings true fulfillment and satisfaction."

www.ingramcontent.com/pod-product-compliance
Lightning Source LLC
LaVergne TN
LVHW091323150826
845673LV00006B/1753

* 9 7 9 8 8 9 0 6 7 8 3 5 5 *